June Bug Versus Hurricane

June Bug Versus Hurricane

Memoir

ERIN CHANDLER

Front Cover Photo of Erin Chandler by Jeff Carson
Back Cover Photo of Erin Chandler by Kopana Terry
Cover Design by Erica Chambers

Rabbit House Press
106 Camden Ave.
Versailles, Kentucky
40383

ISBN-13: 9780692874332
ISBN-10: 069287433X

"Leaning against the railing of a Lake Charles Bridge
Overlooking the river leaning over the edge.
He asked me would you jump into the water with me?
I told him no way baby that's your own death you see.
Too cool to be forgotten, hey hey, too cool to be forgotten.
June bug versus hurricane, June bug
versus hurricane, hey hey..."

- LUCINDA WILLIAMS

For Chan and Daddy

Preface

F or a long time we were lost, my brother and I. Chan, in an oversized passenger seat of Caesar's private jet heading to Aspen, or Vail, maybe it was Reno or Kentucky – he wasn't sure. One leg draped over the other, he wrapped a caramel colored cashmere coat around his long, lean frame and licked the outside of the cigarette paper, sealing in relief. With great ritual, he lit the joint and breathed in deeply, then let a huge cloud of smoke billow slowly out of his mouth, filling the small plane. A few feet away, a shocked and indignant pilot poked his head out of the cockpit. His wide green eyes reprimanded the lone passenger.

My brother smiled at the military grade aviator, "What are you gonna' do… land?"

Meanwhile, in Los Angeles, under illuminated Palm Trees and a blue-black sky, I wore a Paisley mini dress and gobs of purple eye shadow. The Santa Ana winds blew the scent of magnolia mixed with hopes and fears and disappointments of countless sleeping Los Angelinos through floor to ceiling windows. Nico's melancholy voice cast a dreamy pall over a room heavy with romantic, sinister energy.

It was three in the morning at the Villa Carlotta, a dilapidated 1920's building, sort of a Bohemian chic home to the ultra hip and wayward. A handful of Opera singers and leftovers from a bygone era smoldered alongside a new dying generation, across the street from the Scientology center in Hollywood.

Danny lay on the floor with his head propped against the speaker, a smile on his face and tears in his eyes. I inhaled the atmosphere as Nico cooed, *"these days, these days I seem to think a lot about the things that I forgot to do."*

One

"As the son of a son of a sailor, I went
out on the sea for adventure..."

Jimmy Buffett

Las Vegas 1973

"Now Remember what I'm tellin' you, you can't just trust anybody. There are very few people in this life you can count on," Daddy was determined to penetrate our eight and ten year old brains. "Don't be stupid. Don't be gullible like your mother, trippin' through the dew and lookin' out the window."

Fifteen miles from the Las Vegas strip in the Mojave Desert, my father, my brother and I sat Indian style on top of the Red Rock Canyons we affectionately named Gila Monster Mountain. We held our heads high and it was like church. During these ritualistic family outings we couldn't see Vegas or any of the madness from which we had driven. Up there it was quiet and peaceful, the beauty of the place so intense with its striations of red and pearl, miles of flora and Joshua trees miraculously protruding from the from the clay soil. Daddy led us in a rendition of "Put you in the pokey... pa pa pa." I don't know why at eight and ten we were chanting away the police, but we went with it because up on those sandstone cliffs, it was the three of us against the world.

Erin and Chan, Gila Monster Mountain

The sun scorched our skin and the hot wind blew through our hair. I always got the sense we were holding our father up even though he was irrepressible. We talked about how he was going to get back with our mother, about what a jerk our stepfather was and what we were going to do when we were a family again, always preparing for what was just around the corner, the excitement and peace and happiness that was just about to come our way.

"Your mother made a childish decision." Daddy said, "Goin' with a guy that's gonna' talk to her about what: The lifestyle of an ant? That he used to ride a corsair? I mean you talk about Charlie Nobody!"

Daddy, dressed typically loud in pastel patchwork pants and golf shoes, took a sip of his Coors and passed the can to my brother who was perched on the boulder above me.

"Channy, you've got to be the man. You've got to take care of your sister."

Chan reached down for the can and took a man sized gulp, jumped up, knees bent and bouncing and did an impressive impersonation of Bruce Lee. Brandishing handmade nunchuks, wrapped with black duct tape, he maneuvered the sticks, twirling them at high speed under one arm, to the front and side, around his back, then landing them firmly in the opposite armpit.

"You know what it means to call an audible? That's what your Mamma's forcin' us to do. But that's OK. We're gonna' call an audible and change our plan. Like my Daddy always said, if you dig a dry hole, don't fill it up with tears, move your digger! Keep your fist up!" Chan and I held our small fists in the air.

"This is it right here. This is who you can trust." Tears flushed his ice blue eyes and he gathered us up in his arms. "Remember Walkin' Tall? Remember Buford Pusser?" He held up a stick like the one in the movie, the one made to show us life was tough, be loyal to your family and beat the shit out of anyone in the way.

"Walkin' Tall!!" Chan put his arm around me. "I'll take care of Erie, Daddy."

"I love you guys more than anything in the world, your Mamma too. Nothin' is going to split us up. I promise you that. Now keep your fist up!"

We packed up the Kentucky Fried Chicken and climbed back down the mountain, got into our black Bronco and drove in determined silence toward the barking neon strip. By the time we approached whatever hotel or tiny apartment we were living in at the time, our resolve was strong.

In 1973 it was just that, a strip. A garish street populated by eight or nine hotels: The Aladdin, MGM, Sands, Tropicana, Desert Inn,

Riviera, Circus Circus and Caesars Palace, where Daddy worked and we called home.

The valet parkers stood at the entrance and welcomed us through the giant glass doors. The frigid casino air instantly chilled my long, bare, sunburned legs and I winced at the dark, familiar clinging and clanging of the slot machines. Gamblers and guests surrounded my father asking for favors in the form of complimentary hotel rooms, show tickets and casino cash credit.

Chan carried a rolled-up brown sleeping bag under one arm, his nunchucks and basketball under the other. I held the Walking Tall stick and a jump rope slung over my shoulder. We hugged our father goodbye and soldiered through the lobby, heading to the elevator like The Swiss Family Robinson: Vegas edition.

Erin, Dan and Chan Chandler, Aladdin Hotel, Las Vegas

Two

"The young folks roll on the little cabin floor,
All merry, all happy, and bright…"

STEPHEN FOSTER

Kentucky 2003

This Cabin is haunted. I know it is. The walls are saturated with memories of the past. We call it a Cabin but it's more like a men's lodge, probably because of the giant moose head looming over the living room on walnut paneled walls and the swordfish dangling over the giant stone fireplace, fit for a castle. The huge, dark structure has six bedrooms and five baths and an Olympic size pool in the front. It was built for my grandfather in 1936 as a gift from the state and then left to my dad a few years ago when my grandparents died. It's mine now and I don't want it.

My Kentucky isn't the Kentucky of rolling hills and horse farms. I'm a product of a political family. There is a song by Stephen Foster called My Old Kentucky Home, *"The young folks roll on the little cabin floor, All merry, all happy, and bright."* What Chan and I experienced was truly idyllic in the beginning. There was always a sense of royalty, a constant, *remember who you are* from my dad. *You're a Chandler*, he told us. My grandfather,

Albert Benjamin "Happy" Chandler, was two-time governor of Kentucky and U. S. senator. He was the baseball commissioner who put Jackie Robinson in the big leagues and was inducted into the Baseball Hall of Fame. He was on the cover of *Time* magazine with his fist up. This is the legacy we inherited. This is the legacy we had the honor of inhabiting, of revering and oftentimes desecrating.

Kentucky Governor, Albert Benjamin "Happy" Chandler

The Cabin was the epicenter of our eccentric extended family. It was the center of the family's political world. It was in the Cabin where they entertained Elizabeth Taylor and Montgomery Clift when they filmed *Raintree County*. Mamma watched the troubled, alcohol-soaked actor swat off make up artists trying to apply powder to his broken jaw. They later carried the drunk and sobbing movie star to the upstairs bedroom overlooking the pool to sleep.

Elizabeth Taylor and Montgomery Clift with
Mildred "Mammy" Chandler

Jack Lemmon and Tony Curtis visited the Cabin while shooting *The Great Race*. We have pictures of them playing pool with Daddy. Bobby Kennedy called here on a regular basis. Mammy and Pappy sat by the now dilapidated pool with celebrated political and sports figures that found themselves in Kentucky for a rally or the horse races.

Joseph Daniel Chandler and Robert Francis Kennedy

As we grandchildren began to grow up and take over, as we all morphed into our own personal versions of neurotics, the Cabin became a place of transition. We would come here to live from time to time, upstairs in one of the rooms alone, and try to get from one stage of life to the next. The Cabin has witnessed more than its fair share of loneliness and self-destruction, about 90% of which can be credited to my beautiful wreck of a brother.

Life is art. It just depends on what kind of painting you want to do. A lot of us choose a really messy one while others seemingly stay in the lines. I have always been more of a finger painter myself, just throwing in whatever seems right at the time. Chan was creating an amazing piece he called his life, sort of a Wild West or Sicilian Drama. He was not afraid of anything. He was not afraid to die, exploiting every moment of every day the best he knew how.

All the while he enforced his own personal law and punished those who didn't follow... fiercely loyal to his tribe.

I don't know what happened to Chan and me. I don't know if drugs and alcohol "happened to us," or too much need for excitement, but by the time we were teenagers we both went our separate ways, desperately trying to suck every second out of life we could. Every moment had to be filled with something or it was a wasted moment.

Three

"Can't you hear me knockin' on your window,
can't you hear me knockin' on your door..."

THE ROLLING STONES

Kentucky 1985

"Tom Petty!" Chan screamed. He held up my album like some evidence of power and smashed it against the doorframe.

In a small, antiquated room upstairs in the Cabin, on one of the many four-poster beds, I crouched under draped chintz fabric, dodging flying debris. The Stones "Can't You Hear Me Knocking" blared from the stereo, shaking the thin walls. Chan was sunburned and disheveled, aimless and determined in a ripped, button-down shirt and khaki shorts. He destroyed everything he could get his hands on. All six feet three inches of my brother was spitting rage. Here it comes, I thought, the sound and the fury. I tried to be calm so as to incur a minimal amount of damage.

He stormed back into his room and reemerged with a stereo. "You don't want this, do you?" He taunted, dangling it over the windowsill.

"Chan leave me alone!" I tried to save the machine but he hurled it out of the window. For a moment, this appeared to have satisfied his thirst for obliteration, but walking out the door, he tripped over my cat.

"God damn it! I swear to God I'll throw that fucking cat out the window!"

"Chan, calm down," I cried, scared for my cat's life. "Just leave me alone!" He went back in his room and slammed the door. I heard something smash through one of the walls that I assumed was a foot or fist. Then I heard a gun shot.

Chan and Juni Mashayekhi in the Cabin

"Holy shit!" I heard Chan laugh.

"Jesus Christ!" I flung his door open. "What the hell?"

"Relax shitass," he reclined in his bed, revolver close by. "It's a wall."

A few hours later, I looked out the window and saw my brother jumping naked on the diving board. He did a back flip and emerged from the water, Corona firmly in hand. The giant pool was ostentatious enough in the tiny town of Versailles without a naked madman doing flips and swan dives.

Like in a movie, two cops appeared with their guns drawn. They crept around my grandparents' house.

"What are you doing?" I questioned the trespassers. "What are the guns for?"

Chan disappeared inside the Cabin and the cops swiftly followed. They soon drug him out handcuffed and bleeding and pulled him across the yard. As they stuffed him into the back of a squad car, Chan flung his body around and shouted insults at the top of his lungs, "Fuck you, you bald headed mother fucker!"

Arriving on the scene, Mamma walked in circles, trying to grasp what was going on between her children's screams and the flashing lights of the cop car.

Pappy, our 80-year-old grandfather, stood on his back porch steps, red faced and shaking with fury at the grandson who had once been his pride and joy. "Get him away from here!" He yelled from his doorstep. "Get him out of here!"

"You go in the house and shut up!" Mamma roared at her ex father-in-law.

"You can't do this to Mother and Daddy!" Aunt Mimi stormed up the driveway from across the street, yelling at Mamma.

"Don't you say one word to me!" Mamma's eyes were wild with tears.

Uncharacteristically sympathetic, Aunt Mimi hugged her. "I'm so sorry, I am so sorry."

Chan kicked at the caged windows in the back of the squad car and wailed profanities.

"Let him out of there! He didn't do anything!" I lurched toward the cops.

"Back away, Miss!" the redneck cop held his stick up, "you keep away unless you want to go down with him." Stifled, I watched them drive my troubled brother away.

They kept him in an itty bitty, concrete jailhouse on Main Street, downtown Versailles for a few days. When I went to see him, he came into the white cement visitor's room looking so fragile. He leaned over to hug me and I felt his whole body shake. I noticed he was way too thin. Chan acted shy and embarrassed like I was visiting him at his apartment before he had a chance to straighten up.

This was my kind and docile brother, the one that was chivalrous and polite, the one who would run into a burning building to save a stranger. This side of Chan was as prevalent as the madman. The humble, razor sharp charmer with a swagger all his own, the wandering spirit devoid of judgment was a version of my brother I could count on as assuredly as his angry twin.

We sat and talked in what seemed like a pretend jailhouse in a make believe village. We hadn't had a real home in Versailles since we were kids. We didn't live there anymore, but we kept coming back. Since we didn't belong, everything that did took on an illusory quality.

True to form, Chan made friends with his captors and when I left they said I could bring him anything he wanted, cheeseburgers, candy bars, anything. When I returned with a huge bag of food Chan hugged me and kissed the top of my head. "Thank you, Erie."

Four

Los Angeles 1988

I lived so easily in *Laundry and Bourbon*. On stage as Elizabeth in James McLure's play, I was calm and confident, oblivious to the audience as I lived out her/my circumstances. In my head I was no longer in Los Angeles. I was no longer a pawn for its mass insanity under palm trees, the crowded lives and manic freeways. In my head it was a scorching summer afternoon in Maynard, Texas and I could feel the space, I could taste the dust in the air and in my teeth. Everything made sense and I knew my next line.

Then came Jenny in *Love of a Pig*, Velma in *Birdbath*, and Chrissy at the center of *In the Boom Boom Room*. I felt Chrissy in every cell of my body. I was the optimistic, damaged and painfully naïve Go-Go dancer. Night after night, I lived out her life with my emotions. Roles came at strangely appropriate times, when I was that person and understood everything she was saying and doing completely. Each character pushed me through different difficult times in my real life and I emerged with strengths and pieces of myself that I didn't know were there. Chan never found that creative outlet. My brother had nowhere to store the enormous amounts of emotion he had bubbling up inside.

In the protective bubble of the theatre, I expressed all the love, exuberance and anguish that I had pent up. Instead of being made to feel inappropriate, I was praised.

Erin, early Hollywood headshot

I got it into my head early on that I was going to be a big star. I thought by going this route, I could bury myself in other lives. I would be protected from the outside world, shielded by theatres and movie sets and people would be nice to me because of what I was doing. However, fashioning a career where people watched every move you made, I was making some pretty sloppy moves.

I was nervous, neurotic and obsessive/compulsive. Getting out of the house, I said aloud, "off, off, off, off," checking every burner and candle, each window and door. I even counted when I felt exposed in my hipster neighborhood in the Hollywood Hills. Sure I was about to trip all over myself, I mumbled under my breath, "one, two, three, four, five, six, seven, eight, nine….".

For years, I had one of the most hard-core acting teachers in town, Robert Carnegie. Bob believed you shouldn't step foot on the stage unless you were a real actor. He never intimidated me because he knew, and I knew, I belonged there. In a city where all you have to do is get your picture taken and copied a bunch of times to be considered an actor, he maintained an intense integrity based on his studies with the legendary Sanford Meisner at the Neighborhood Playhouse in New York. You had to live, breathe, blush and feel everything. And I did.

Erin Chandler and Dale Dickey in Del Shore's play *Daddy's Dyin' Who's Got the Will*, Theatre, Theater, Los Angeles

When Michelle, from the William Morris Agency, approached me backstage after a play, she gushed, "I looked at Naomi and said, who is this person? Why do I not know her? Honey! I was blown away... we have to talk." It seemed my Hollywood dreams were coming true.

Back in my apartment that night, I discovered a long, syrupy, southern message from Naomi Judd on my machine, "Michelle looked at me and her mouth dropped. And Darlin', she has seen everything!" Naomi went on about my performance, how impressed and excited she was for my future, and how happy she was to be there in the beginning, "honey, I want to take you to dinner before you're famous."

Her daughter, Ashley got on the phone. We had been friends since our days in the theatre department at the University of Kentucky. "If I just got a message like that, I'd be ecstatic!" she said.

We went to dinner the next night at Chaya Brasserie in Beverly Hills to celebrate my upcoming success. Naomi was an angel as usual, Ashley was cool and confident as usual, I was slightly uncomfortable as usual.

I didn't trust that it was happening because this had happened before with other agents and managers. "Honey! You should have your own show. You remind me so much of Holly Hunter or Mary Louise Parker or Drew Barrymore or as the Eagles put it, *"we're gonna' take care of you, dahlin', we're gonna' make you a movie star."*

I smiled and thanked them, feeling glamorous and confident in the theatre, on my turf. But in the cold, stark offices of their turf, I didn't fare as well. After hours of getting ready and putting on the perfect flowery dress and curling my hair and doing my nails and putting on my make-up just so, suddenly, I wasn't so confident. I was nervous and anxious and they had the upper hand.

Consequently, after a long meeting of trying to figure me out, and a lot of fawning and smiling too much on my part, the ax dropped. "Honey. I just don't think we can start a whole new career right now. We have so many people to push already and to take on an unknown right before pilot season!" Lunacy, I'm sure.

I drove up Wilshire Boulevard sobbing, feeling like every cell in my body would explode. I ran up to my apartment, tore off my frouffy dress and scrubbed off my make-up. I sat at a glass table in the kitchen by the window, poured a glass of wine, took several deep drags of a cigarette and tried to forget about it. The dark side of my newfound aspiration in wildly cutthroat and ambitious Hollywood revealed a deep-seated insecurity.

The view from my window on Iris Circle in the Hollywood Hills looked over to the houses encrusted in the mountains across Caheunga Pass. The populated hillside and the freeway below had once been a dirt trail where Rudolph Valentino rode horseback to his favorite watering hole, the Knickerbocker Hotel. I could see the famous landmark that also served as the backdrop when police dragged Frances Farmer through its lobby half naked.

I tried to forget about the whole place. I tried to forget about its tragically glamorous past and its dog eat dog present. I didn't want to play the game. It made me feel fake and foolish. Kissing ass didn't come naturally. It wasn't in my make up. But I wanted it all so badly. I wanted everything they had to offer behind those shiny Paramount gates, even if they did drag me out of a hotel kicking and screaming in the end. I still wanted it. My biggest fear was remaining anonymous and insignificant.

Erin Chandler, Leslie Jordan and Mark Pellegrino,
publicity shot for *Lost in the Pershing Point Hotel*

Five

*"Let him know that you know best, cause
after all you do know best, try to slip past his
defense without granting innocence... "*

THE FRAY

Los Angeles 1990

Chan showed up at my apartment in West Hollywood with a Corona in his hand, a gun in his pocket and a very scared 21-year-old Pat Wilhoit by his side. Pat, our childhood friend from Kentucky, had a frozen, kidnapped gaze on his face and his blonde curls were dripping with sweat. He seemed to be trying to tele-pathically convey an SOS. I knew the drill.

"Hey kid!" Chan breezed passed him and hugged me tight. He looked sun kissed and handsome, a little drunk but happy to be in his element, an open destination road trip. Chan was rarely in Los Angeles, which added to his excitement. Sunshine and beautiful people always make for a good first impression, no matter how many you have.

I was glad to see my big brother but my body immediately switched to high alert mode. I could see by Pat's expression that Chan was on a roll and there was no putting the brakes on. My pretty friend from acting class was over and Chan quickly honed in on her. Victoria was a real California girl. She starred in movies and TV shows known for parading women around in short shorts, showing off tan legs and firm bodies. I knew he would be attracted to her but Victoria was tougher than the Kentucky girls he was used to and he seemed naïve, grinning and wobbling around.

Joseph Daniel "Chan" Chandler, Key West, Florida

Chan sat on the couch, opened a safety deposit box and emptied out its contents. He had just retrieved the stash he kept at a bank in Santa Monica. What fell out were a few gold chains, a chunky 14-carat bracelet that said Freedom, a Rolex watch and several shiny coins. It was his bold statement laid out in front of Victoria, promising a good time.

"Come to Vegas with me," he winked.

"Oh, I don't think I can do that," she said suddenly shy.

"Come on, come to Vegas with me," he flirted.

"I don't… I don't think I can do that." She glanced over at me and giggled. She was clearly flattered but not sure what to make of my mysterious brother who had hijacked our afternoon rehearsal.

"Chan, she doesn't want to go and you shouldn't either," I called out, still at my precautionary post by the door.

"Kid, when I want your opinion, I'll ask for it," Chan said, pulling a Corona from his duffle bag, followed by a bag of pot and a gun, which he placed next to him. He wore a T-shirt and khaki shorts. His eyes were glassy. I was helpless at the other end of the room but strangely fascinated with the ritual to come, the joint rolling process I had seen my brother perform a million times before.

I knew I had zero control of the situation. If Chan wanted to go to Vegas, he was going to Vegas. If Chan wanted to take my car to Vegas, he was taking my car. If Chan wanted to take me, then I was going to Las Vegas. I observed the situation with a familiar apprehension that had taken root and settled deep into my being a decade before. This unease, this not knowing how the day will play out, this waiting for the ball to drop, quite literally waiting for the gun to go off, had come to define my earthly experience as much as anything else.

On the other hand, this was fairly new to Pat and he was exhausted from his cross-country trip with Billy the Kid. Apparently Chan had gotten into numerous bar brawls along the way and it seemed he was just getting started.

"You don't have to go with him," I said to Pat. "You can go home."

"You don't have to go with him…" Chan mocked me in a baby voice, spinning his gun. "You can go home."

"Don't you think it's a little dangerous for you to be driving?" I asked my brother.

"Don't worry about me kid, I'm packin'," he smirked, alluding to his firearm.

"What are we, in the wild west?" I asked.

"What are we, in the wild west?" he repeated in the same baby voice.

"I really just want to go home." Pat whimpered.

"You can stay here like a pussy if you want," Chan taunted. "But I'm going."

"Chan, brother-man," Pat bowed his head, "I really just want to go home."

"Hey kid, can I use your shower?" Chan ignored him and jumped up, infused with new energy.

"Sure," I said.

He grabbed another Corona and strutted toward the bathroom.

The moment he left the room I called his AA sponsor, Ernesto. Chan had been in and out of the program for years and developed a close relationship with his sponsor from when he lived in Marina Del Rey and religiously went to AA meetings in the Valley. I pleaded with Ernesto to get right over to my place, reporting that Chan was in town and had a big gun. I was petrified he would get into a fight and someone would tackle him and shoot him with his own gun. He was obviously out of control, pitifully swaying back and forth with that childish grin plastered on his face.

By the time Chan got out of the shower, Ernesto was over and had confiscated the weapon. He came out of the bathroom in a cloud of smoke.

"Hey buddy!" Pulling off a casual greeting, Chan brought Ernesto in for a warm embrace, "what a surprise." He shot me a dirty look." Man, I'm just out the door… but it's good to see you!"

Then putting in one last bid for the girl, "Victoria, you wanna come with me?"

"No," she whispered and smiled, "I don't think I can do that."

Victoria eventually went home and Pat got on the next plane to Kentucky. Chan made it as far as Palm Springs.

"Hey kid," he said in a high, stopped up voice.

"Hey, where are you?" I asked him.

"You gotta' come and get me," he said.

"What?"

"You gotta come pick my ass up. I just got the shit beat out of me by a bunch of redneck mother…"

"What?" I interrupted.

"Just forget it, I need you to get in the car right now and drive to Palm Springs.

"What?"

"Just don't ask any questions," he snapped, softly, angrily. "My nose is fucking broken, I got rolled. They stole my Rolex, my jewelry, all my money."

"Who?"

"I just stopped off to play basketball with these guys. I swear, kid. I just wanted to have some guys to play basketball with and I got rolled. I got blood all over, Jesus Christ!" I could see him at the pay phone. I'd seen him beaten up before and it made me sick.

"I can't come this second. I'm afraid to drive by myself." I wanted to help him but didn't know how.

"COME AND PICK MY ASS UP!" he screamed.

I was frozen with fear. I knew I would get there and Chan would knock me out of the drivers seat and drive me God knows where. Plus I had already had a few drinks myself by this time so I wasn't going anywhere.

"Chan I can't drive right this second!" I screamed back.
"FUCK YOU!" He hung up.

He made it to Las Vegas and called me the next night.
"Hey kid, how are you doin'?" Chan said. "I'm at Caesar's, I just got out of Chicago. They were amazing." He said about the band.
"Who are you with?" I asked.
"Nobody... man, I wish you were here. You would have loved it. I had to leave in the middle of the show because I was starting to cry. I miss her so much kid," he cried into the phone. "I can't stand it, I miss her so much."
He was talking about a great love he had recently lost. Lissa had broken up with him just prior to this particular jaunt across country.
I could hear the slot machines and the lonely, sick atmosphere of the casino. I thought about my brother, alone in the Caesar's Palace showroom where we had spent so much of our childhood. I thought of his insides being infused with the overpowering horns and minor notes of one of our favorite bands.
"Chan, go home, please go home. Are you driving?" I was suddenly panic stricken, sick with worry listening to his sad voice cracking.
"No, I'm walking. You would have loved the show," he sniffed, sounding a little better. "Remember that song we love? I'm so lonely Erie, I'm so sad," he wept into the phone.
"Chan, please go home. Please... maybe... call an A.A. person." I regret saying that but I didn't know what to say.
"I'll see you later kid." He hung up.
I let him down, he called to talk to me and I told him to go find a stranger. I thought maybe someone there could help him. I

spent the next hour calling him, leaving sobbing messages on the phone at our dad's empty condo. I prayed like I had never prayed before or since, begging my guardian angels to team up with his and safely follow him home. I walked with him in my mind's eye from Caesar's, all the way up the strip, to our dad's condo behind the Hilton. I visualized angels above his head. I wept from my bedroom, begging God not to let him die or get hurt. I wailed and prayed until finally he called.

"Hey kid… I'm fine," he said sounding completely normal. "I'm home. Don't worry Erie," he laughed. "I'm fine."

I hate Las Vegas.

Six

"Give me love, give me love, give me peace
on earth, give me life, give me life..."

GEORGE HARRISON

Burbank, California 2003

I was tired of Hollywood. I was tired of pushing. After twenty
years in Los Angeles, my skin was paper-thin and my sense
of self had all but disappeared. It was my idea to move back to
Kentucky and into the Cabin. I had always chosen to stay as far
away as possible but suddenly Kentucky loomed large in my mind.
The lush, green, rolling hills of Versailles, my hometown, seemed
the perfect place, in fact the only place, to heal my nervous blood
from the quagmire life out West had become.

The move seemed all the more appealing because I didn't have
to go back alone. I was married by now and had a partner with
whom to dip into the valley of the past who understood my present. My husband was also an ambitious artist so it was like taking a
bit of LA with me. I didn't have to let go of my extravagant dreams,
just put them on the back burner. Most importantly, I had someone
to shield me from my overwhelming family, who in my mind *was*
Kentucky.

Sam was a singer, songwriter with shaggy brown hair and ice blue eyes who had come to Los Angeles by way of Montana and Seattle. He had a practiced cool so integrated into the fiber of his being, you would never have known that his dreams, like mine, were as vital to him as breathing. We had lived together harmoniously for five years before he proposed to me on a mountaintop in Butte, Montana under Fourth of July fireworks.

Erin's country wedding 2002, with friends Matt Flanders and Connie Blankenship, Kentucky

But two years into our happily ever after, our creative world became a world of *where is the pay off?* Our flailing careers were at a standstill and the plays we had done, the movies, bands, albums and all the excitement that transpired was replaced with endless telephone calls with publicists and agents about hype and look, what we should be doing and what we were doing wrong. We were both fragile, insecure and finally broke.

On New Years Eve, 2002, Sam and I curled up beneath a heap of blankets and pillows on the floor of our house in Burbank. The heated pool shimmered and steamed outside and like a couple of kids, we ate popcorn and drank cokes watching my childhood in Kentucky flash on the small screen via old 16mm films.

Chan and Erin, 156 Elm Street, Versailles, Kentucky

"Look how cute you are," Sam said. My three-year-old self wobbled about, copper ringlets poking out from under an over-sized football helmet. I passed the ball underhanded to my five-year-old brother. Chan, in full uniform, shook his silky, dark hair while running backwards, doing quarterback-style maneuvers.

We watched Chan and me march through a colorful pile of leaves under two large maples in our front yard on Elm Street. Our Irish Setter, Irish, standing by. There were films of Easter egg hunts with the neighborhood kids. I wore a white pleated wool dress that barely skimmed my bottom with a matching sweater and an Easter hat with a long, yellow ribbon. Chan wore a little green suit with white knee socks. He put his arm gently around me and pointed out the colorful painted eggs to fill my pink woven basket.

The 16mm films captured Daddy in his pajamas on Christmas morning playing bongos and shooting toy guns. Our father jumped in and out of the mini toy castle while Chan and I smiled under mounds of wrapping paper. There was Christmas Eve where Mammy and Pappy held court at either end of their long mahogany dining table. Mamma had me dressed in a short, red velvet dress with white stockings and Chan, in another little suit. He always seemed the most energetic of the crowd, running circles around the table where aunts, uncles and our three cousins Ben, Whit and Matthew sat. Josephine and the other cooks bustled about with trays of stuffing, collard greens and oyster casserole.

Father and son at home, 156 Elm

It was almost unbelievable that the charmed family we watched on the small screen was my own. Kentucky looked deep and fresh and wholesome. My mother looked like a movie star and my father looked strong and happy and healthy. I went to sleep that night filled with sweet memories.

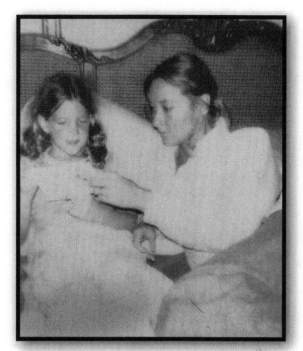

Mother and daughter at home, 156 Elm

"I think we should move to Kentucky." I said the next morning, New Years Day, 2003. "Like… this week. Live in the Cabin rent free, save up some money and then when we're ready, move to New York!"

Sam looked up from his guitar, "Okay."

And like my landlord, Rose Marie Welch, an eccentric opera singer who wore tiaras and ball gowns well past the days of performing, always said, "and so it is!" And so it was.

That familiar feeling of getting up and getting on filled my stomach with a nervous, happy energy. My sweet spot, like Chan's, was high on change and out on a limb with no idea what the future held.

The next day while Sam holed up in his recording studio wrapping endless black cords around and around and around before placing them carefully in plastic crates, I packed up the rest of the house. I hadn't taken a breath by the time my cousin, Whit, flew in to join us for the cross-country drive. Whit just so happens to be one of my favorite people on the planet. He has an uncanny ability to see the big picture and possesses the sort of even temperament that is incredibly comforting. Whit has a way of not taking life too seriously and in his presence I tend to follow his lead. This has always made him my go-to relative in times of uncertainty.

He lives in the ivy-covered house in Versailles where he was raised and runs the family owned paper, *The Woodford Sun*. His hyper intelligence comes from his dad, my father's brother Ben, and his artistic talent was a gift from his mom, my Aunt Toss. I used to think he would fit in perfectly with the free spirits of my Beachwood Canyon neighborhood of Los Angeles, with his black turtlenecks, Beatles mop top hair and penchant for being most alive after midnight.

Unfortunately, when I finally got him to the West Coast, I couldn't get away fast enough. The moment he arrived, I announced we had five days, then we were out of there. I was so ready to leave I was practically gone. I could barely stomach another day of pretentious Sunset Boulevard. Ventura, Santa Monica and Hollywood Boulevards seemed dirty and boring to me.

In spite of it all, I tried to be a good hostess and dragged Whit from site to site. It seemed essential for him to experience the stars on the Walk of Fame so I pulled up to the curb of the Mann Chinese Theatre so he could jump out and see Marilyn Monroe's handprints and Humphrey Bogart's footprints. We went to Malibu and I showed him Pepperdine University, where I studied Theatre and Dance. We had dinner by the ocean at Gladstone's and then took him to see the Griffith Observatory. Finally, Sam drove him down Sunset and through the neon glare pointed out the spots where people had died.

All the while I turned to face him in the back seat, talking animatedly and a hundred miles a minute about how glad I was to get out of there. I told him that we couldn't wait to get on the road, we were ready for a change, we were really stuck in a rut, running like rats on a treadmill, we needed a rest in Kentucky then we could go on up to New York.

When we were finally on the road and out of town, I calmed. I exhaled and my body released an internal sedative that made me want to weep with relief. The pressure was off and the clock stopped ticking. We leapt off the train going nowhere and landed in a field of daisies. We had been rescued and were smiling and holding hands from our stretchers.

"The West is not the best!" we chanted.

We spent our first night on the road in Sedona, Arizona and I woke to a sign. A bright yellow cross of light rose behind the mountain with a long line of shocking bright blue down the middle. The light of the sun burst behind these beautiful red mountains and made a perfect star.

"I think this really is the psychic vortex," Sam said pulling me close from behind, his cheek against mine. Whit came out in his pajamas and stood beside us. He didn't say a word, just looked out over the layers of multicolored mountains. How perfect it seemed to begin a new chapter in this majestic place, like a prayer.

Erin and Sam on the road, Sedona, Arizona

After the warmth and good vibes of nature's stunning desert beauty had fully pierced our beings, we decided to do the touristy thing, which in Sedona is to see a psychic. Right after breakfast we went on a hunt for the perfect spiritual insider. There was quite a selection. Mystics on every corner offered psychic readings, aura photography, astrology, vortex tours, Reiki, energy healing and hypnotherapy. We walked through several crystal hanging, Shiva-selling gift shops until we ended up at the Center for New Age.

A large woman at the counter with long gray braids, tube socks and Birkenstocks handed us a book of soothsayers.

"There's over twenty to choose from." She said with a wide yellow smile. "Take your time. Flip through and let me know."

Whit chose Victor, a tall, skinny hippie with a marble colored ponytail. We called him Merlin. Sam picked Kelly Lynn, a sweet, cheerful, housewife-looking woman. The name of my guru of choice escapes me but I remember she had thick raven hair and a witchy, Renaissance fair vibe. I'll call her Esmeralda.

Esmeralda arrived first and rushed me out of the gift shop. As I slowly climbed the stairs, she kept looking back, curious and all too aware of my fragility. She led me to a dark room with a small window and we sat down at a card table. She smiled briefly, insincerely, before spreading out the tarot cards.

"It doesn't look good," Esmeralda came out of the gate with darkness. "It's like you're jumping out of the frying pan into the fire."

That's not possible, lady, I screamed in my head. The tough part is behind us. This is a very positive step!

Esmeralda's cell phone rang and she jumped up and crossed the room to turn it off. She looked out the window and said she was waiting for someone to pick her up for lunch. It sounded like a lie. Begrudgingly, she continued with the reading. Then steadily let out one nasty detail after another that she saw in my future.

"How are you and your husband?" Esmeralda asked, shaking her head like she didn't want to tell me what she was seeing.

"Wonderful," I said. "That's the one thing in my life that's been absolutely... wonderful."

"I see you in a storm," she warned. "You will fight and think about splitting up. I don't know if you will, but you will think about it."

"We've always been crazy, happy together and completely in love." I panicked.

"You will have many money problems. It will get much worse before it gets better. You are on fire inside. I see fire burning inside of you but you are using it the wrong way." Her hocus-pocus voice was thoroughly cliché and would have been funny if it weren't so scary.

"You will be working with a healer in Los Angeles."

"But I'm not going to *be* in L.A." I said. "I'm going to be in New York."

"New York will be really bad if you go there now. Things will start to get better around next Christmas but you have a lot to go through before then."

It was January. Things will get better next Christmas? I couldn't take any more bad news, and I sure couldn't take another bad year. I wanted her to finish. I wanted to get up and bang on the window, yell at Sam and Whit to come get me. I wanted to throw money on the table so she would shut up. I stumbled down the stairs and got in the car.

I slammed the car door shut, relieved to be back in my rolling home sealing me away from Esmeralda's doom. Sam nodded his head toward the empty storefront of the Center for New Age.

"I think Whit's in there getting cloned."

At that moment my cousin came bopping out, following Merlin to the cashier. Whit had his hand on Merlin's shoulder and they were smiling and laughing like old high school buddies.

Approaching the car he dropped the act, slid slowly in and said in his southern drawl, "I'm not sure I can sit, I've just been... in the ass."

Merlin charged him two hundred dollars for what amounted to nutrition advice, don't eat dairy and keep away from fast food. Whit was too polite to make a fuss.

"My guru said I've been teaching classes to the Crystal Children on another plane while I sleep," Sam piped in, feeling spiritually superior.

For the next few hours we talked about our psychics. The consensus being that I was way too sensitive for the negativity that spewed from Esmeralda.

"She really got to you didn't she?" Sam asked shaking his head. "I knew she would. It's a scam. They're frauds. It was a gift shop! Honestly, she didn't know what she was talking about. Do not let her get to you, please."

"Yeah," I said.

"Oh no." Whit teased. "Merlin was right on the money."

Unexpectedly a need to prepare myself for a cold winter in the Cabin crept up and I became obsessed with finding a pair of cozy moccasins. I requested that we stop at every Indian reservation we passed. I was on a mission, yearning for comfort in the form of fluffy shoes. Each place seemed to have better ones and by Winslow, Arizona I had bought four pair. Sam panicked. He was sure I would spend all our money before we even got to Kentucky.

"We have stopped three times in the last fifteen miles and we are never, ever going to get there!" Sam screamed.

Driving into New Mexico, we sang with John Denver, "*Ohhhhhhhh I am the eagle...*" We listened to Julia Darling and John Lennon and David Bowie's *Hunky Dory*. Looking out the window at the passing communities and ever-changing terrain, Route 66 seemed like one big music video.

Texas took the longest to get through, with its endless stretches of nothing. Sam asked if I wanted to take a detour down to Lubbock, where I went to Jr. High and High School. I didn't.

We made it across the country in three days. That first night in Sedona, the second in Albuquerque, and our third and last night in a shithole in Tulsa, Oklahoma, room 161.

On our last day we were totally and completely exhausted. We stopped at a truck stop café called Whitmore Farm for their amply advertised catfish sandwiches.

"Can you feel it?" Sam asked stepping outside the car. The wind blew grey, cold air and we quickly wrapped ourselves in scarves and jackets. "The epicenter of the trip."

"The heart of America," Whit said zipping up and looking out over the wind-chilled land.

"We're further than the center." I protested.

"I'm not saying we're halfway there, I'm saying this is the epicenter of the trip. When you think of this trip, you will think of this place and time."

"I'm gonna have a hard time getting the hipsters out of my mind," Whit said. "The psychic vortex... my guru."

"What was your guru's name?" I asked Whit. "Gabriel... Raphael?"

"Beelzebub?" Sam laughed.

"His name was Robert Tilton," quipped Whit.

I gazed out the window as we zoomed through Missouri and dipped into Mississippi. The same road that consisted purely of desert now featured snow-covered forests on both sides. The sky was black when we crossed a bridge over a dark river and I had a tiny pit in my stomach when I realized we were in Louisville, Kentucky, only one hour away from our destination.

At nine p.m. we pulled into Versailles, silent but for the gravel under the car wheels up the driveway to the Cabin. My cousin Matthew, Whit's younger brother stood on the front porch to greet us.

Matthew had started a raging fire in the giant stone fireplace and a six-pack of beer was on the table. I suggested we stand in a circle and pray. Turning my face to the ceiling, I closed my eyes and summoned all the forces of peace I could conjure.

"This is the beginning of letting go officially and starting the next phase of life, in the most calm fashion we possibly can." I said. "And I feel really, really good."

At that precise moment, in front of the roaring fire, George Harrison sang from the music channel on the big screen TV, *"Give me love, give me love, give me peace on earth, give me life, give me life…"*

Seven

"Papa was a rolling stone, wherever he
laid his hat was his home..."

T<small>EMPTATIONS</small>

Kentucky January 2003

"Glen Frey!" Daddy screamed. "One of the nicest guys I know." He pointed his cigar at a picture on the wall of himself with the Eagle, toasting Coronas and laughing.

"A rock-n-roll star, but more than that, a serious wordsmith," Daddy strolled down the hallway in his boxer shorts, preaching, "and if American literature is rock-n-roll, which a lot of people say indeed it is, he is one of the foremost exponents of American Literature. He has the feel of the pulse of a human just about as well as anybody."

Dan Chandler and Glen Frey, Aspen, Colorado

Much to our surprise, after thirty years in Las Vegas, my father had decided to come *home* too. Weary of the corporate new order that was swiftly turning his old world Vegas from a high class, exclusive adult playground into a tourist spot for the t-shirt and flip-flop clad masses.

I knew what was coming, a barrage of cigars, Scotch and sports figures. There would be strangers walking in the house at all hours of the day and night, helping themselves in the kitchen and the bar. There would be yelling on the phone, parties and endless campaigning for my cousin Ben, who was running for governor that year. This was absolutely not the calm, countryside gazing, lightning bug watching evenings I had been dreaming of.

Over the past several years, my relationship with my Dad consisted of having lunch or dinner once a month when he was in LA. We met at the Palm or the Bel Air Country Club and spent the afternoon rehashing our lives over bottles of Chardonnay. He was warm, loving and gregarious, singing, laughing, grabbing my hands and hugging me. Then came the part where he told me everything I was doing wrong. He praised, criticized and taught, reminisced, gushed and strategized. All of this was interspersed with big plans for the future. After three or four glasses of wine he got confrontational, mean and insulting. If I disagreed, which I always did, I was a "fuckin' idiot!"

We usually had an audience of two or three of his friends, who sat quietly, drinking their vodka, eating liver and onions and watching the show. I always left these soirees, drunk and in tears, with a wad of money in my pocket. The thought of doing this in the Cabin on a regular basis sent shivers down my spine.

"Erin Lynne, my little angel." Daddy flopped on the couch and hunched over his cigar and glass of Scotch. "I'm so mad."

"About what?" I asked.

"That your Mamma left me." He spoke as if it happened last week, last year even, not thirty years ago.

"Her mother and daddy were just getting a divorce at the time," my father chomped on his cigar, "boxes all packed and set to go, she was embarrassed by that so I think she was ready to make a pick. And of all the people who were dating her, George Carey, the president of the Idle Hour Country Club, some other guy Patterson, very successful guy, both after your mother and she picked me, but I don't know…"

Dan Chandler and Lynne Bryant Chandler on their wedding day

"She loved you, she still loves you, that's why she picked you," I said the words with the same conviction I had delivered them a million times before.

"Ahhh no. No, she was probably dazzled by the governor's mansion. Hey! The world's made of bullshit so you can't say. Bullshit's important! It is an important sales tool."

"She loves you," we carried on like two actors in a long running play. "If she didn't love you, she wouldn't still be talking to you every day now."

"Oh, well now," he hung his head down low. "Now we're just looking out for each other. The wagon's... the wagon's in the circle."

"She loves you. She loves you more than anything." I repeated. That was the honest truth. In spite of her disappointments and romantic cravings Daddy still maintains the biggest space in her heart.

He took a puff off his cigar and a long pull from his drink and with a mouthful of ice he summed it up, "it's just at this stage of the game, I don't give a damn how dumb she was. I'm gonna try to protect her from herself the rest of the way. 'Cause she's Polly Put Upon! She wants to set up Molly Pitcher's nursing home and personally look after every human she can find."

"Mamma loves you." I said before delivering the kicker, "she just loves you in God's way."

"Well, she doesn't have to," Daddy scoffed. "I'm just sayin,' I'll keep the Indians away, that's all. And she's been fightin' and it's been a bitch! She wanted somebody to look at her, and this is the price she paid. The devil must have said, 'Okay, this guy is going to pay attention to you and NOTHIN' else. And when you leave the room he's gonna hyperventilate!'

My mother had a different take on marriage to my father, which she has shared with me through the years:

"We were walking into the Maddens' or the Whitneys', one of them," Mamma recalled of the socialite's gathering. "They were having this ball under a huge tent. I was all dressed up in this gorgeous, long, pink dress with pearl beading. There were men in tuxes and white gloves holding umbrellas because it was raining.

We stepped out of the car and I remember thinking, 'I don't ever want to do this again.' At that very second your father looked at me and said, 'I never want to give this up!'"

"We lived that public life for so long that it became less and less about us, and more and more about careers and other people." Mamma defends her decision to dismember the tribe. "I kept asking him for more private time, more dinners by ourselves, not at the Idle Hour Country Club. We would drive toward Lexington and I would say, 'Please Dan, just this once, there's this new little Italian place on Versailles Road, let's go there and eat together and talk, just the two of us.' And your Daddy would say 'Okay' and then drive directly to the Idle Hour."

Dan and Lynne, Lexington, Kentucky

The Idle Hour came to represent all that was phony and pretentious about Lexington. My mother, from old Kentucky roots herself, hated Lexington society. Before I could even form an opinion, she drummed into us the falseness of the very thing in which Daddy bathed himself. There are countless stories about the eccentric privileged community that both of my parents were born into. There is a deep-rooted, impenetrable hierarchy of old-money families that inform the temperament of this world steeped both in old English tradition and over-the-top decadence. Books and magazine articles even pontificate about the extremely wide gap between the upper and lower classes due in large part to the horse industry and the wealth attained and sustained through breeding and racing of Thoroughbreds that dates back to pre Civil War times.

Chan and I were born into this closely sealed society. Although not recipients of huge trust funds or heirs to massive amounts of land, we are beneficiaries of the love and respect bestowed upon our grandfather, which gave us somewhat of a free pass in our old Kentucky home.

I remember watching my mom get ready to go out in our house on Elm Street, frantic and hurried, smelling wonderfully and looking beautiful with streaked blonde hair and big froofy hairpieces. She ran up and down the stairs in long skirts and sequined tops. I recall the sound of her heels clicking on the brown and ivory tiles. My Marsha Brady babysitter stood by the stereo putting on a record, while Mamma gave Marcella, our live-in maid, instructions. *"If lovin' you is wrong, I don't want to be right,"* came through the speakers and like clockwork, my stomachaches would start. Upstairs in the window seat overlooking our front yard, I leaned into the pale wooden shudders and cried. Mamma hugged me, and ran out of the house, leaving me with all these strangers. I sobbed for a good hour or so.

Another memory comes rattling through my body. We are at the Kennedy Bookstore in Lexington next to the University of

Kentucky campus. It's raining buckets on one of those cold, gray and black afternoons. Mamma and Aunt Leigh are walking through the aisles wearing wool skirts just above the knee and high-heeled boots, their silky frosted hair wrapped in colorful scarves. They were the most beautiful, smart and fashionable women I had ever seen. I stared out the window onto the slick black street and heard Paul Simon singing over the loud speaker, *"My Mamma loves me, she loves me, she gets down on her knees and hug me. Oh she loves me like a rock."* I look back toward the fluorescent aisle of college books and am overwhelmed with the most awesome sense of loneliness.

Mamma was happy with Daddy sometimes because I remember her laughing and laughing. They enjoyed music and the theatre together. They hung out with singers like Rosemary Clooney and went to Basin St. East in New York and listened to Ella Fitzgerald at the height of her career. They saw all the latest Broadway Shows and afterwards dined at all the most famous restaurants, Sardi's, 21, Copa Cabana and The Stork Club.

The sixties were a very glamorous time for my mother and father. They were invited to have breakfast with President John F. Kennedy in his hotel room when he was in Louisville, Kentucky.

"Oh, I didn't know there was a lady joining us," the President smiled. "Let me put a jacket on."

Mamma was stunning to look at and projected the kind of tranquility and composure that drew men like flies. The president was no exception. When he held her hand and stared into her eyes, she said she could tell immediately that the rumors of his philandering were true.

"He was extraordinarily handsome and very, very charming!" Mamma blushed remembering. "He opened the door wearing the whitest T-shirt I had ever seen!"

"It wasn't Fruit of the Loom!" Daddy laughed. "He was a good-lookin' guy, and I'm tellin' you, there wasn't an ounce of fat under that T-shirt either!"

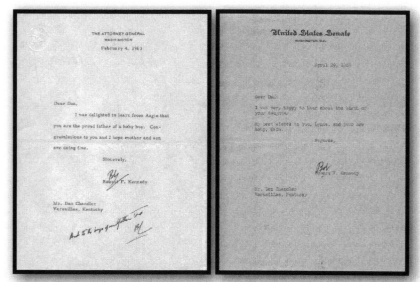

Notes from Bobby Kennedy re: Chan and Erin's births

The friendship with the Kennedys had been going on throughout JFK's political career and my father developed an especially close bond with Bobby. My grandfather contemplated running for President at one point and then Vice President, which was the basis for that particular meeting in Louisville. Daddy dabbled in politics and ran for Congress, but it never took. A lifelong affinity for skirting the law kept him from being a serious contender.

Eight

"Ay ay ay ay, take this waltz, take this waltz…"

LEONARD COHEN

Miami 1968

By 1968, Daddy's new business venture, running the concessions at the Jockey Club, took us to Miami Beach. We kept our house on Elm Street but drove south to live in an apartment in the hotel, which was still under construction. The condominium tower overlooked the bay and a harbor of yachts and sailboats. Walter Trautman, the Georgia-born playboy and business tycoon who built the Jockey Club had emotionally adopted my impetuous father, and in turn, was named my godfather.

Walter looked like James Bond ascending the spiral staircase of his opulent two-story penthouse, where we swam in the indoor pool. The posh opus was at the center of Miami's burgeoning social scene and featured a restaurant, three bars, a giant swimming pool and tennis courts. It was the hotspot for the Jet Set. Sports legends like Australian tennis star Rod Laver and golfer Arnold Palmer hobnobbed with the likes of Jackie Gleason and White House Press Secretary, Pierre Salinger. How Daddy came to own three apartments there had something to do with investments and holding companies, phrases as mysterious to me as I'm sure they were to the men investing and holding.

Chan attended kindergarten in Miami at The Little Red Schoolhouse, next door to the Jockey Club. Mamma walked him down the long driveway of the lavish hotel and delivered him to the front door. My mother and I wore matching Lanz gowns with small red roses. We made homemade Christmas ornaments on a glass table next to the balcony. Through the window we could see a bridge covered with lights that sparkled, reflecting on the dark blue water. During the day Mamma, tanned and fit, took us each by the hand and we walked beneath the coconut trees along the edge of the bay while Daddy spent time with Walter and an ever-expanding circle of dazzling guests.

Dan and John Wayne, Jockey Club, Miami, Florida

My parents had very different views on parenting. Daddy, a lifelong and fearless thrill seeker, let Chan get on some daredevil's back to climb a high circus tower set up by the pool. Throughout the long climb, Mamma begged my father to make Chan come down. He laughed and ignored her, giving the stranger the go ahead to climb up and up and up with my brother. When they got to the top, he proceeded to do a back flip off the tower and into the pool with Chan clinging to his shoulders. Terrified to tears, Mamma describes the feeling of turning to stone at times like these, which became more and more frequent.

Shopping and hobnobbing with the Jet Set did little to assuage her growing doubts about the relationship with our father and things went downhill fast. A never-ending social life was not what she had in mind for romance. By the time we were back on Elm Street, their marriage had disintegrated.

"He would bring people home with him and turn on both the stereo and the TV, then get on the phone. It became really, really hectic," she says. "There was no communication between us. I did a lot of cooking and cleaning up and a lot of entertaining."

I'm taken aback with these claims of cooking and cleaning. For the life of me all I remember are TV dinners, chicken pot pies and McDonald's. She tells me, in all seriousness, "well, it was probably before you could eat."

Mamma gets a mix of nostalgia and guilt. After years of Chan and Daddy flogging her with the idea that she ruined our lives, she still wonders if everything is her fault.

"We fixed a beautiful little pale yellow room for you with windows looking out into the trees," Mamma says dreamily. "I hand-painted your dresser with wildflowers all over it. You were so feminine, so unlike Chan. He had been so strong and masculine, and you were so delicate and it was perfect."

"Lynne wanted to be happy and I just didn't think it was that important," Daddy jokes.

My father's behavior, nowadays referred to as alcoholism, was another contributor to the dissolution of their union. My parents'

Christmas Eve together he went to a party and left my mother to put out the legendary Santa Claus spread on her own. She filled the living room with balloons, streamers, toys and packages. Around midnight, Daddy stumbled up the walkway and narrowly made it to the house. Mamma opened the door and watched her husband as he started up the steps, then passed out on the landing. She stepped over him and went to bed. To a thirty-three year old romantic, this was a living hell.

Incarceration in the summer of 1971 didn't help either. Daddy was audited by the IRS and found guilty of tax evasion. Actually, he was most guilty of massive disorganization and ignorance of tax laws. My father was a whirling dervish who didn't question lawyers or accountants, assuming they would 'handle it.' His attention was forever directed toward whatever hit the pleasure button of the moment.

The Federal Government took the opportunity to make an example of the Governor's son and put him in the Louisville county jail for three months. Mamma drove an hour from Versailles to Louisville to see him every day. Daddy's friend, eccentric Lexington club owner Jimmy Lambert, sent him a steak dinner every single night. Not surprisingly, my gregarious dad made friends with his captors, like Chan would in the future. The cops came to love him so much that upon departure they gave him an honorary police badge. When he was released it was all backslaps and hugs for 'Dan the Man.'

Nine

"But if this ever changin' world in which we live in,
makes you give in and cry, say live and let die..."

PAUL MCCARTNEY

Las Vegas 1973

"Chan, Erin, this is Darby... Darby this is my little Erin and son Chan." Daddy held us out like a prize she just had won. "Darby baby, if you need anything at all, call the Sports Book. I'll be with Lem. They'll know where to find me. Be back in a few hours."

Career opportunities in both Kentucky and Miami had diminished for Daddy so when Cliff Pearlman, the president of Caesar's Palace in Las Vegas, offered him a job as a casino host he jumped at the chance. They had become friends while they both had apartments in the Jockey Club in Miami, playing tennis together and running in the same circles. With my parents officially separated, Mamma returned to Kentucky and Daddy headed to Vegas. Chan and I now had two very different homes.

Chan, Dan and Erin, Caesar's Palace, Las Vegas

Las Vegas was a world of adults and we were expected to keep a low profile. Our babysitters were the secretaries, showgirls, and cocktail waitresses caught unawares as we were hurled toward them.

Darby was the first person I had ever seen with a tattoo. It was a little rose on her ankle. Darby was like most of the women around at the time, young and pretty with ambitions of climbing the hotel and casino business ladder. In my father they found a mentor, a tour guide and a comedian. Inevitably, she and the other ladies came to realize that their fun times with Daddy would be temporary because Mamma, Chan, and I would forever come first. The good news for them was that life without my father would be infinitely less stressful. There was nothing easy about him. As exciting as his company could be, it was his way, it was unpredictable, and it was fast as lightening.

"Dan, I have to be...." Darby reached out.

"You know where to find me!" Daddy yelled over his shoulder.

"Dan, I was just on my way..." she said weakly.

"I'll take care of it!" He called out the window of the Bronco, leaving the three of us staring at each other.

"I'm sure he'll be back soon." Chan broke the silence.

"Do you... have you all eaten?" Darby smiled. "Do you like pizza? Let's order pizza."

We all surrendered into what would surely be a long visit.

"How about I put out some blankets and pillows and you all make yourself at home until your Daddy comes back."

The next day Daddy didn't show up, but a long black limousine did. In fact Chan and I routinely had a chauffeur-driven limo taking us from one deliciously gaudy station to the next. This made us not altogether unpopular kids to babysit. The fringe benefits were many.

The truth is most of the time we didn't have anyone watching over us. We were left to our own devices, loosely guided to certain stations where we were to wait for our father to collect us (an exact time was never foreseeable). The number one go-to spot most summer days was in front of Caesar's swanky restaurant, The Bacchanal. We sat patiently on the ornately carved chairs day after day, hour upon hour upon hour. L.P.—low profile, was the mantra drummed into us. We were just that while we had a front row seat to the comings and goings of the casino. Ladies passing by teetered on the red and gold carpet, sipping margaritas in white crochet bikinis, mesh skirts and high heels. Casino bosses with giant stomachs in three-piece suits puffed on cigars and plotted their next move.

Erin and Chan poolside, Las Vegas

"Hey kids, where's your old man?" One such casino boss, Ron Collier said, approaching our chairs.

Ron was a round, bald car salesman before Daddy managed to get him a job as a pit boss. He obediently followed Daddy around the casino and they prodded and teased each other like grade schoolers in a tawdry schoolyard.

"Hello, Mr. Collier." Chan quickly stood and gave a firm handshake.

"Why aren't you kids out by the pool?"

"Daddy's about to get off and we're going to Red Rock Canyon," Chan said.

"Tell him I'm looking for him, will you?" Mr. Collier headed back toward the casino.

"I think he's in the Baccarat pit," I offered my two cents on his whereabouts.

The operator came over the loudspeaker calling after our father for the thousandth time: "Paging Mr. Chandler, Mr. Dan Chandler."

Caesar's Palace publicity shot with their new
Vice President, Dan Chandler

Like many cultural waves you can't predict, Las Vegas in the seventies was a particularly exciting moment in time, an exclusive grown-up playground. Until the early eighties, the men who created Las Vegas ran nearly every hotel, mobsters like Cleveland bootlegger, "Moe" Dalitz, Al "Mokie" Faccinto, "Wingy" Grober, and "Marty" Buccieri.

"I do my own killin'," said Benny Binion, another no nonsense, hardscrabble pioneer of the gaming industry. The owner of Binion's Horseshoe took a shine to my father from day one. This big bear of an imposing figure wore a giant hat and bolo tie and he always seemed to be part of our day. Daddy loved the fact that Benny was a poor Texas kid who went from horse-trading, to liquor running, to dice dealing and arrived in Las Vegas just after World War II with a couple million dollars cash in suitcases and his extended family piled into a Cadillac.

"Wake up," our father shook us awake at three in the morning.

"What?" I said in the darkness.

"Come on, we're going to Binion's."

"Erie, get up." Chan pulled at my arm, half asleep.

We hurried out of our beds and into the long empty hallway of The Carriage House. The fluorescent lights revealed the velvet, pale gold, and paisley walls of the nearly vacant high-rise apartment building that stood at the end of the strip. Turns out a money collector had threatened Daddy and we were forced out on the lam. I wasn't frightened. In fact, I got a charge out of the adventure. Even now, when all hell breaks loose, I am washed over with a strange calm.

Binion's Horseshoe was a step down from the marble hallways of Caesar's Palace. Downtown Las Vegas was seedier, dirtier and the high stakes gambling was just a little more dangerous. But in our hour of need, this is where we fled, and Benny protected us from the bad guys.

"What's he doing?" Chan and I peered through the banister, sitting on the staircase of yet another gaudy red paisley carpet. Our father was below in a sea of blackjack tables talking to a couple of men in suits.

"He's getting us a room," Chan said, putting his arm around me. "Don't worry."

Daddy looked up and held his fist up with a smile. We in turn held both our fists up through the banister.

Soon after this, we began a new ritual called "The Money Dance," chanting and bouncing from one foot to the other like Indians. We never told Mamma about these shenanigans, never wanting to blow Daddy's cover and ruin his chances for reconciliation.

My father was enthralled with the psychology of the gambling racket. All of the drama fascinated him. There was always something untoward going on. The whole town was built on it. There were several hits put out on his buddy Ash, whom we saw on a daily basis. Once eight sticks of dynamite were strapped to the bottom of his car. Ash was shot by an anonymous gunman leaving Caesar's Palace. So was Edward "Marty" Buccieri, another floor man at Caesar's, who was shot in the head in his parked car after working at the casino since its inception. They say Chicago mob boss Joseph Aiuppa ordered his murder.

Frank Sinatra famously ran his golf cart through the glass doors of the Sands hotel after being denied further credit by casino owner Howard Hughes. This melee was stopped only when Carl Cohen (old school wise guy and Hughes henchman) knocked out two of the superstar's front teeth.

The Frank Sinatra my dad hung out with was a proud grandfather. Nancy had his first grandchild that May of 1974. After Sinatra's midnight performance at the Circus Maximus Showroom in Caesar's Palace, Daddy would rope off a section of the lounge and get a bottle of Frank's favorite drink, Jack Daniel's No. 7. Frank would pour his own and talk to Daddy about politics, the human psyche, his romantic conquests and his recent run ins with bad press. They shared a love and respect for mutual friends, NFL stars Joe Namath, Kenny Stabler, and Billy Kilmer. Both held high regard for those men's men who knew their way around a football field.

At Piero's another famous wise guy hangout, Daddy stood up to greet a dark skinned, well-dressed man heading to our table, "how are you, sir?"

"What a pretty little girl you are," the heavy-lidded stranger said, leaning over to kiss the top of my head.

"Thank you." I smiled with a slight lisp.

"Thaaaank yeeeew." Chan mocked me.

"Even the nicest guy you know could be leading a double life," Daddy leaned in and whispered when the man was out of earshot. "It's never a good idea to know too much. The ones that do are usually next in line on the chopping block. That's a guy you don't even want to be on his good side."

Chan and I trained our eyes on our father, averting them from the fellow in the leisure suit settling into a round table in the center of the room. A woman at his side sparkled vacantly in a bedazzled turquoise turban. It did not escape either of us that we were on his good side.

Save for the occasional drop off to a stranger's house, it was a glitzy and glamorous life with our father. We had carte blanche at every coffee shop, restaurant and boutique in the desert town. Anything we wanted just took a signature. Chan got a job setting up lounge chairs and bringing people towels out by the giant sapphire pool while I sat in the sun and ordered club sandwiches like they were going out of style.

By the time I was eleven I had discovered high fashion at the Caesar's boutique Hot Cha Cha. It had an Aspen/Palm Springs, disco feel with racks of rhinestone flared hip hugger jeans, velvet tops and jackets made of silk ribbon. It became my haven.

"Hi Cutie! You been out at the pool?" The sales girls said knowing full well I was about to drop hundreds of dollars on some sequined pants or feather hairpiece.

"Yes. My dad said he would meet me here if I found something," I said, heading toward the most flamboyant of articles.

"How is your dad? I just love him!" Everybody did.

"He's fine. Working a lot," I said with a smile.

"Well he sure is a character!"

I picked out several different outfits that would make Cher proud and set them on the counter. I paged my dad and he faithfully appeared, flirted with the sales girls and broke out his ever-present wad of money. He plopped the cash down on the counter as I gathered up my clothes. Then he walked me to the Circus Maximus Showroom. We walked beyond the velvet rope, down the side of the music hall and through the kitchen to backstage.

Dan presenting Tom Jones with Kentucky
Colonel Honor, Caesar's Palace

The opportunity to hang out backstage and befriend the entertainers who performed in the showroom was another perk of being a casino host and a huge bonus for Chan and me. Tom Jones, Sammy Davis Jr., The Lennon Sisters, Steve Lawrence and Eydie Gorme, Paul Anka, and Glen Campbell were all among our new set of friends. They all had standing gigs at Caesars, which meant I had a better place to perch than the Bacchanal chairs. Andy Williams was his closest entertainer friend. He played Caesar's for two weeks every few months so we got to know him very well. Daddy was quick to saddle his backup dancers with the duty of watching over me. It was electrifying to watch my babysitters get ready while the orchestra tuned up. In return, Daddy provided them with complimentary dinners after the show at the lavish restaurant of their choosing.

From across the long dressing room mirror I could see back up singer Trish's beautiful brown skin shimmer. She smiled at me across the room with her big eyes while applying more silver shadow and adjusting her costume. The bell-bottom pantsuit she was poured into had slits all the way up the side, making it easy to eye her strong dancer's body. Her partner Gloria stood beside her, a long alabaster leg stretching across the make up table. One arm reached to pin a blonde hairpiece into her thick flaxen hair while the other secured a belt on her doeskin bell-bottoms. Gloria winked into my reflection when she saw me light up at the spectacle that was their lives. 'Slither and Hook' they called themselves. Life was a Cabaret.

Erin Lynne Chandler

"Where is he? Listen," Gloria said with her ear to the speaker for Andy's cue. "Shoot we gotta' hurry…"

"OK, Doll, we gotta go down," Trish said to me with a kiss before running down the spiral staircase to the stage.

"You gonna watch from back here or go around?" Gloria asked.

"I think I'll run around front," I said, glancing in the mirror at my own glittery lids.

"See ya' after, sugar," her figure slid down the stairs as fast as Trish's.

I dashed around to the front of the showroom and the maître d ushered me to a round table in the front row, complete with a red tablecloth and shiny silver ice bucket, bottle of champagne protruding out. It was my favorite spot because I could rest my elbow on the pulsing, illuminated stage, literally feeling the magic. Just then Gloria and Trish appeared under the spotlight and at the microphone to hit their music cue.

The song was "MacArthur Park," and Andy sang, *"I don't think that I can take it/ 'cause it took so long to bake it/ and I'll never have that recipe again!"* prompting Gloria and Trish to belt out, *"Oh Noooooooooo, OOOOHHH NOOOOOO!"* Night after night, they never let him down. Their voices were perfectly pitched and powerful, booming throughout the place.

Daddy would sneak in during the middle of the performance and sit with me to watch the show. Nothing made him happier than people like Gloria and Trish. He was always more impressed with the back up singers than the main attraction.

"Look at that!" Daddy let out his big raucous laugh, wiping his wet lashes. "You think they're havin' fun?"

Ten

"Send lawyers, guns and money, dad get me out of this…"

WARREN ZEVON

Las Vegas 1977

A few summers into our tenure in Las Vegas, Chan and I met our life long best friends. Leader was the son of El Paso criminal defense attorney Lee Chagra, a Lebanese-born professional gambler who would drop several hundred thousand at the blackjack table at any given moment. Lee looked like a Middle Eastern J.R. with his white leisure suit, big mustache, cowboy hat and thick gold chains.

Dan Chandler and Lee Chagra (wearing cowboy hats) with guests, Circus Maximus Showroom, Caesar's Palace

"Erin Lynne, this is your Uncle Lee," Daddy said when he first brought Chan and me up to the Chagra's suite at Caesar's.

"Nice to meet you," I said.

"Nice to meeth you," Chan teased, emphasizing my little baby voice.

"This is my son Chan."

"Hello." Chan gave him a firm handshake.

"This is Leader... little Lee. You boys are about the same age, aren't you? How old are you Lee?"

"Fourteen," Leader said.

"Me too!" Chan said, "wanna go play the slots? I know some that are hidden from the security cameras."

"Sure," Leader said, and they were off.

It was customary for Caesar's Palace to send a jet to pick up the entire Chagra clan and bring them to Las Vegas, an advantage for anyone who traveled with trunks of cash. The Chagras were a tight-knit family that rivaled the Corleones, legendary for their flashy lifestyle and outlaw ways. Lee's brother, the infamous drug kingpin Jimmy Chagra, was on the scene at the time. He held court in the casino with a gaggle of prostitutes dripping in jewels. Jimmy was known to do such unspeakable things that even his own family had a hard time warming to him. Still from 1970-1979 he was one of the biggest gamblers in Vegas, bringing footlockers packed with millions that he stored in Caesar's casino cage, courtesy of my father.

By anyone's estimation, Chan's new friend Leader came from an unconventional family. The Chagra brothers were notoriously steeped in drug running and other criminal activities. Jimmy was head of possibly the biggest marijuana smuggling operation in the world in the 70s. He brought freighter ships and private planes filled with pot into the country. The Chagras paid off cops and politicians and had their own mafia of gangsters.

Criminal defense attorney, Lee Chagra, El Paso, Texas

Daddy's new best friend, Lee Chagra, had a reputation as a powerful criminal defense attorney who kept his own clan as well as a slew of other ne'er do wells out of prison. He also held an infamous ongoing high stakes poker game at his home in El Paso. Leader grew up in this fortress complete with hidden cameras, beefed-up security, massive rooms with safes of cash and mounds of cocaine and marijuana. The house was also an atmosphere that sustained an extremely close, religious family. His big sisters were beautiful, high-spirited teens. Their mother Joanne was always on hand as a loving and nurturing caregiver. Chan came to respect and envy the Chagras' steady, undying devotion to each other and over time Joanne Chagra developed a deep love for Chan.

The day they met, Leader asked his mom if he could go with Chan over to our place behind the Hilton. With Joanne's permission, Daddy sent the two boys in a Caesar's limo to our condo on the golf course. Chan immediately took Leader back to our father's room and pulled out a gun from the top shelf of the closet. The young boys examined the 357 Magnum and tried to impress each other with their knowledge of the weapon.

"Have you ever smoked pot?" Chan asked him.

"Sure." Leader said, though he never had.

Chan reached into a pocket of my father's dress shirt and brought out a little bag. The two struggled to roll something resembling a joint then headed outside and lit up on the golf course. They spent the rest of the day riding their skateboards around the gated complex until dusk. When the limo pulled up to take Leader back to the casino, Daddy still wasn't home. Leader looked out the back window and saw Chan waving goodbye with a big smile on his face. Leader said he couldn't help but feel sorry for his new friend because it was getting dark and he was still by himself.

I was probably at the other end of the gated complex with my new best friend, Juni Mashayekhi. Her father, Kamran Mashayekhi was another professional gambler my father befriended. Kamran worked as a reporter for the Shah of Iran and when that country's Empress-Consort, Farah Diba visited Kentucky, Daddy went through Kamran to get a picture. Then he offered his Caesar's business card and said to come have fun in Las Vegas. Kamran did come with his wife and kids, over and over and over until they finally moved there. Such is the allure of gambling and the charm of Dan Chandler.

Kamran had already hustled his way from Tehran to London, to the Swiss Alps, to Mclean, Virginia. He had an outlandish personality and would strut across nude beaches in St. Tropez, all 110 pounds of him, white as snow, naked except for his black socks and black briefcase. He was well aware of this hysterical spectacle and got a kick out of embarrassing his kids. He was loud and spoke with a heavy Iranian accent an inch from your face. Kamran worshiped his kids and showered them with everything he could get his hands on.

Mr. Mashayekhi also threw lamps across the room and flailed his diminutive self around hotel rooms spitting profanities in Farsi, "Kesefat Koon nashhoor! Koskesh Jende!!" Which translates roughly into 'you dirty piece of shit, unwashed ass, slut, whore.' On more than one occasion during a family dispute, Juni and I locked ourselves in the lavish bathroom and plotted a bus trip to Kentucky while Mrs. Mashayekhi opened the door and screamed down the hallway, "Security!! Security!!"

This was just a day in the life of the Mashayekhis and I was along for the ride. Whether it was Disneyland, or Hawaii, or water-skiing on Lake Mead, they let me stay in Juni's room for weeks, even months, at a time. It became a running joke how I lined all my duffle bags neatly against the wall. Daddy provided free rooms, complimentary dinners at the finest restaurants and front row seats to see Elvis and Tom Jones. The Mashayekhis provided highly dramatic babysitting services.

It was so much more as Juni and Leader became family. Leader and Chan were like brothers and Juni and I were like sisters. We learned to play the guitar, took dance classes and made up a secret language that we still use today.

Coincidently, like the Chagras, there were also filing cabinets full of cash in the Mashayekhi home. While there was always talk of gambling at Leader's house, Kamran's daily bet was also hovering in the air. While Leader's house made mention of mob hits and drug lords, in Juni's home there was conversation of would-be assassins and kidnappings by Iranian officials.

It's hard to explain the depth and breadth of influence the Chagra and Mashayekhi families had on our lives. It's hard to know when my father started snorting enormous amounts of cocaine with his new crowd, or when he began hiding millions of dollars in the walls of our tiny condo for Jimmy Chagra and receiving an easy $20,000 cash for this covert service. It's hard to know when he began traveling to Guatemala City with Jimmy and Lee and Uncle Brad, meeting Guatemalan officials under the auspices of opening a casino. I'm not sure when Uncle Brad was hired on as their security, and it's hard to decipher when they began doing business with the drug running, machine gun culture and flying them to Las Vegas in the Caesar's jet.

Dan Chandler and longtime love, Delores Halloran, Las Vegas

Suffice it to say that only a few years after the friendship with the Chagras started, the high life of the seventies was about to come to a close. On July 25th 1978, Lee Chagra was shot to death behind his desk in El Paso. Jimmy Chagra was sent to jail for plotting the murder of Federal Judge John Wood, who was set to preside over his drug trafficking case in San Antonio, Texas. Their brother Joe was sent to jail for the same case and Jimmy's third wife, Elizabeth, went to jail for delivering the $250,000 paid to the hit man, who happened to be Charles Harrelson, father of actor Woody Harrelson.

Uncle Brad, who was working jobs for the CIA at the time, was sent to prison for ten years on drug smuggling and weapons charges. His partner Drew Thornton jumped from a plane wearing a bulletproof vest, Gucci loafers and a green army duffel bag with 40 kilos of cocaine, $4,500 in cash, two pistols and a few knives. His parachute did not open. This scene was so infamous in Kentucky that it would be the subject of the book full of unsubstantiated facts, *The Bluegrass Conspiracy*. It also become an episode of Dominick Dunne's *Power, Privilege and Justice* and inspired a storyline for the television show, *Justified*.

I know my father had nothing to do with these darkest of actions. Daddy adored Lee and was devastated by his murder. He brought him several times to the Kentucky Derby and the audacious lawyer charmed my grandparents and all of my father's friends. Daddy wasn't close to Jimmy like he was to his brother, but since Jimmy dropped $800,000 on an average night at the 'store,' it meant he was a customer and my father's responsibility.

My mom said seeing Uncle Brad, her baby brother, exit the private jet in a leather jacket and cowboy boots trailing behind Jimmy Chagra, made her sick. She pleaded with my dad, "If you love him, you will get him away from those people."

"She didn't know we were trying to get closer to Jimmy," Uncle Brad smiled. "He was our way in. The target was Nicaragua but we had to get by the Guatemalan officials first."

It was all contacts in Antigua, Taser guns, hookers who were informants, Bowie knives and machine guns, drugs and drug dealers and trunk loads of cash. It was lawyers, guns and money. My brother watched and learned from the masters.

Eleven

*"Well it's full speed baby, in the wrong
direction. There's a few more bruises if
that's the way you insist on heading…"*

ALANIS MORISSETTE

Los Angeles/ Las Vegas 1988

I was sitting alone in my apartment on Sycamore when the phone rang. "Hey kid," Chan said, out of breath.

"Hey, what's goin' on?" I asked.

"I swear to God, Erin, I think Daddy almost had a heart attack."

"What?"

"Fuckin' Scott man."

"What?"

"Fuckin' Scott is being such a dick and I told him to get the fuck out of my house and he wouldn't leave so I went and got my fuckin' gun and I pointed it at him and said, 'Get the fuck out of my house!' and Daddy came in and I swear to God kid, I thought he was gonna have a heart attack. He came in and freaked out. He leaned back and almost fell over."

"Chan! Why are you pointing a gun at Scott?" I spat, wondering what planet he was on to point a gun at one of his best friends.

"Fuck you," he said and hung up.

The next morning Daddy drove Chan and Scott to Palm Springs and checked all three of them into the Betty Ford Center. Chan stayed for a week and left. My dad stuck it out for two weeks. He said they let him leave early because he was such a model patient. Scott stayed the whole month.

Chan overdosed once. I'm not sure what he was on. Daddy told me. It was the day of the Breeders Cup, Saturday November 2nd 1991. Chan saved the clipping, this tiny square of newspaper that I found in his briefcase:

"Police get a chance to take it easy: Police had a quiet day at Churchill Downs yesterday, especially compared with Derby Days. One alleged drunk and twenty people charged with scalping tickets."

One alleged drunk! One? That was Chan. Out of all those millions of alcoholic Kentucky drinkers swilling down their mint juleps, bourbon and wine, Chan was singled out as the one drunk.

I found out later that he had passed out. I remember seeing pictures of him looking so handsome as his day started, in a blue suit, eyes just a little droopy. He must have taken something really heavy after that, God knows what and what combination, but he passed out and the ambulance came. They took him to the hospital and pumped his stomach.

I can see it as if I was there now and it breaks my heart. Seeing him all dressed up, sitting on the floor of Churchill Downs, propped up by the wall with hundreds of bloated drunken preppies stepping over him. It makes me sick, him being so vulnerable.

I overdosed once too, but it doesn't break my heart, it just tugs at it. I was partying with a few people in Lexington and we were drinking and smoking and doing cocaine (which I hate!). Anyway, I walked by myself down a long hallway and suddenly my whole body started shaking and convulsing. I had on this long peach sweater that went to my knees. My body threw itself into the door of this bedroom and my sweater got caught on the doorknob. I was thrown onto the bed in the empty dark bedroom and as I was shaking, I kept breathing and saying, "I'm okay, I'm okay, I'm okay." And finally I was.

Twelve

"Where have you gone Joe DiMaggio, a
nation turns its lonely eyes to you..."

SIMON AND GARFUNKEL

Kentucky January 2003

"I was born at the top and clawed my way to the middle!" Daddy laughed.

Actually, my father's spirit was absolutely unconquerable. According to him, there was never any way to go but forward, and not just forward, but forward with a good attitude. Having such a famous father would cast a shadow on any young man, but Daddy was a life force that surpassed even my grandfather, especially in the joy department.

Daddy had entered the University of Kentucky on a basketball scholarship and played on Coach Adolph Rupp's undefeated basketball team. Although he ran eighth man on the twelve-man squad he was the crowd favorite. Everyone cheered for Dan the Man and jumped to their feet when the 'dark horse' was handed the ball. From then on, my father contributed his fighting spirit to Coach Rupp.

"I know other athletes who were similarly ground in the Rupp mill and the end product was a man built to stand any measure of stress that life might deal him." Daddy wrote in his book, *From Both Ends of the Bench*. "They were warriors. For him it was as General George Patton said it should be. The only proper way to bow out is 'By the last bullet of the last battle of the last war.'"

In spite of his own personal giant spirit, Daddy spent his life promoting the father he idolized. But my grandfather was much more of a figurehead than a hands-on father. Pappy's head was in politics and baseball and achievements rather than parenting. He lived in Washington, DC and traveled the world during Daddy's youth so my father was shipped off to a boarding school in Arizona when he was eight. It was 1942 and he spent several years at the Little Outfit before attending one year at a Military academy that he hated. The bulk of his education was spent at Darlington in Georgia where he went for six years and graduated. In between semesters and holidays he traveled to Europe with his mother and joined his father for impressionable events like Babe Ruth's funeral.

Babe Ruth's funeral and pitching ball with Ty Cobb in the front yard of the Cabin were experiences so essential to the way Daddy saw the world. He never wanted the last place representing the glory that once was to change. The Cabin was a shrine to my grandfather and he wanted it to stay that way.

The place hadn't had a makeover in decades so in order to start fresh, for it to feel like a home, Sam and I pulled out all the stops. We swept and dusted and mopped until the floors shone. I took down Pappy's old law books and scoured the floor to ceiling bookshelves, then filled the shelves with a colorful new library of ideas. The threadbare Oriental rug was thrown into the shed and swapped with a bright orange shag. Mammy's old chintz curtains disintegrated with the tiniest tug, so they were replaced with brand new drapes. We exchanged the uncomfortable buckle couch from the forties with our giant Moroccan sofa overflowing with pillows. My red velvet chairs added a Parisian flair next to the stone fireplace.

"I had a head start with Daddy. I had a head start being Daddy's son," Daddy continued the history lesson mid makeover. "I had a head start all the way and I carried that out to Las Vegas. Being Daddy's son has never hurt me, your Aunt Mimi railed against it, it helped her. It helped Ben, gave him the Woodford Sun and a place to stay home."

Sam nodded respectfully. Daddy dropped into the Moroccan couch, holding his scotch up high so it wouldn't spill.

"Pappy integrated organized baseball by lettin' Jackie Robinson play," he began to school Sam in our history, "when *specifically* Kennesaw Mountain Landis, the commissioner for 22 years before Dad, *specifically* would not let blacks into the organized baseball… into the major leagues."

He took another mouthful of ice and scotch, "my dad, when the vote was fifteen to one of sixteen major league clubs, Dad sided with the one and made him the majority and ok'd bringing Jackie Robinson in. So he was not afraid to go against… because he was the Czar. He was the Commissioner. He could do anything he deemed was in the best interest of organized baseball. And he deemed it being in the best interest, not only of organized baseball, but of life in the United States."

And as if that was not enough he ended the lesson with this, "he signed 38 death warrants in eight years as governor in Kentucky."

My father had his own wall of fame down the long hallway of the Cabin, which was always entertaining to me. He had a slew of classic Vegas shots with Frank Sinatra, Clint Eastwood, Hank Williams Jr. and Jimmy Buffett, even John Wayne and Joe DiMaggio in Vegas. My absolute favorite was the Caesar's publicity shot from 1975: Daddy dressed in a toga being fed grapes by scantily clad cocktail waitresses in Roman inspired costumes.

"Erin Lynne, my baby! This place looks just terrific. It's never looked better." Daddy said finally noticing all the work we had done. "We've all been away from home too long. Sam? Do you know what a little angel my baby is?"

"Yessir," Sam choked. "She's an angel."

"Where is that picture of Kenny Stabler? Daddy said suddenly searching for anything out of line. "Sam?"

"I don't know," he said. "Maybe Erin put it in the closet."

"I know I had a framed picture up here of Sir Karmen SuKampto and Pappy."

"I don't know…" Sam said.

"Ben's right, if you don't nail it down Erin'll throw it away."

"I didn't throw anything away Daddy! I'm just fixing it up for the first time in ages."

"I liked the way it was." He pouted.

"Well, it's gonna look better than it ever has."

"Who is that woman on the mantel?" My father studied the black and white photograph over the fireplace. His eyes bulged with disdain at the image of my great-grandmother on my mom's side, Muwee. She wore a gorgeous beaded gown and feather hat circa 1920.

"Daddy! That's Muwee. That's my great Grandmother. Dear's mom."

"Nobody cares about the house of Muwees mom! Sam, tell her."

"I didn't know we were living in a museum," I said.

"Erin Lynne, you have absolutely no sense of history." Then shuffling back toward his room he changed his tune. "You do what you like. This is your house. My little angel."

Around my dad, I have always felt like Gilda Radner's abused child character on *Saturday Night Live*. Flipping her head back and forth, pushed and pulled by her oblivious parents, finally comparing herself to a roll of tape.

Uncle Ben and Matthew broke the monotony when they came over to muddle through the trash I set outside.

"You don't want this?" Matthew leaned over a broken-down toaster.

"No," I said. "Do you?"

"You never know Erin Lynne," he smiled in all seriousness. "I'm a bit of a pack rat."

"This is Mother's," Uncle Ben said, holding up an old mildewy blanket.

"I know, it's gross," I said, putting down another large box of mismatched glasses.

He turned to his son, my cousin, and shook his head, "Matthew, help me take all this down to the basement. We'll go through it later."

With that, they gathered up the mounds of plastic hangers and broken, clouded vases, ancient, unwound cassette tapes and clothes of God knows who and took it all across the lawn to the basement of Mammy and Pappy's house. In other words, adding it to the pile of crap they will never look at again. We are a family of serious hoarders. I escaped that trait and became the punch line, "if you don't nail it down, Erin'll throw it away!" Uncle Ben laughed, crossing the yard.

Thirteen

*"From the Halls of Montezuma
to the shores of Tripoli..."*

U.S. MARINE CORPS

Farmington, Maine 1976

"I guess there's no chance of you becoming a decent human being," my stepfather said.

Paul Knipping was a tall, gray-haired health and biology professor. He had been a Marine fighter pilot in World War II. He wore beat up jeans, sweaters and a leather bomber jacket. Dr. Knipping rode a Harley and talked about flying corsairs, tapeworms, Schistosomiasis and his pet tarantula. Mamma thought he was fascinating because he was the polar opposite of the Idle Hour Country Club and everything she was running from. They took long romantic drives by the river in his VW convertible. He adored our mother but resented the hell out of the fact that my brother and I came along with the package. In turn, Chan resented the hell out of this man inserted into our lives.

Nevertheless, after just one year of dating, our 35-year-old mother married 54-year-old Paul August Knipping in a small ceremony at a country church. Chan and I were in Las Vegas, not fully aware of what was taking place. After the summer with our dad, we joined our mother in the small picturesque town of Farmington, Maine. Paul had left his previous position at the University of Kentucky and taken a job at Farmington College in New England.

Increasingly resilient fifth and seventh graders, we quickly made friends. Chan played on the basketball team and earned the nickname "smooth." I spent days with my friend Tammy, who lived in the trailer park in the field behind us, and Amy, a Mormon who lived up the street with ten siblings and a most unusual father. Afternoons, I dutifully helped out in our homemade assembly line, stacking wood under a shed. The snow drifted all the way up to the top of the house, burying the surrounding cars and lawns with a white sheet of shiny ice. Icicles stretched from the rooftops all the way to the ground.

Our house was a sweet old-fashioned cottage at the end of a dead-end street. It was built in the 1800's and had no insulation. There was a wood burning stove in the kitchen and fireplaces in every room. At night we piled onto the green corduroy couch that fit all four of us and watched *Welcome Back Kotter* and *Barney Miller*. We were only a few minutes from the town's ski lift and went skiing almost every day. Chan and I may have started with snow plowing on the bunny slopes, but we were slaloming down the tallest mountains before the season was through.

Mamma, looking a bit like Sadie Thompson with her platinum blonde hair and high heels, held my hand as we window-shopped downtown. She was out of place in the small village, wearing a skirt and form-fitting cashmere sweater. I saw a pair of blue shoes in the window that I wanted.

The woman at the counter had on men's pants, a quilted coat and a hat with earflaps. Her head was down.

3

3244

45

"My daughter would like to try on those shoes in the window," Mamma said.

The woman refused to look up.

"Excuse me. There are a pair of navy shoes in the window and my daughter would like to try them?" she repeated.

The woman kept her head down. Mamma grabbed my hand, put her head up and marched toward the door.

"Let's go Lamb, we'll find a better pair in a nicer place."

Before I could bask in the magic of my first slow dance or figure out what the mysterious rolled cigarette was that Chan brought home from school, we were moving again. The long cold winter and rigid people got to the newlyweds. Paul got an offer to teach health and biology at Texas Tech and they extended an invitation for Mamma to work in the mental health department and continue her education. As Chan and I were heading back out to Vegas for the summer, the truck with all our furniture was on its way to Lubbock, Texas.

Fourteen

"This is not real, this is not really
happening. You bet your life it is..."

— TORI AMOS

Lubbock, Texas 1977

Sitting on a stoop outside Del Estrada, our beige and tan duplex, I looked out over the dirty, brown desert of the Texas panhandle. I was twelve years old. Lubbock was dusty, really dusty and really brown, no trees just tumble weeds and swirling dust devils. The wind blew dirt in the air that got in my hair and teeth. With nothing better to do, my friend Jan and I snuck up the street and around the corner to Chris Osborne's house. He was our cute seventeen-year-old neighbor who blared Aerosmith's *"Walk this Way"* and Queen's *"Fat Bottom Girls."* He gave us beer, and taught us how to French kiss on his stairwell. He kissed me, then kissed Jan, then kissed me again.

I spent as much time as I could away from home. My stepfather dominated our environment in Lubbock. The furniture and books, the china and photos were recognizable, but the judgmental, disapproving presence of Paul made this shaky territory for Chan and me. He sang, *"From the halls of Montezuma to the shores of Tripoli..."*

forever reminiscing about flying in Squadron 214. When I passed him in the kitchen he shook his big professor head and sneered. When I offered an opinion at the dinner table he scoffed, "I'm not gonna' listen to some infant!"

Paul had a horrible temper and was mean as a snake more often than not. He was sullen, hostile, dismissive, and verbally abusive. Everything in his eyes said he was barely tolerating our presence. The motion of a backhanded slap met any indication of disrespect. Paul didn't spend time with his own grown sons, so he certainly had no use for Chan and me. He dreamed of whisking Mamma off to some remote destination and came close to accepting teaching positions in both the West Indies and Barrow, Alaska.

"Children should be seen and not heard," he said time and time again.

As we fluctuated between the unrestricted life in Las Vegas and the police state that existed in my mother's house, the two worlds could not have been more different. It was a hard pill for Chan to swallow that Paul was in our lives for good. The turmoil continued to escalate.

"That's my father's chair you are sitting on. In fact, all this furniture is my father's!" Chan screamed at our step-dad.

"Chan, sit down," Mamma said.

"Buddy, why don't you sit down and cool off."

"I don't have to listen to you, you're not my father!"

Chan came over to the table, took the full plate of food Mamma had prepared for him and hurled it across the room. The red plate shattered against the wall. Roast and mashed potatoes oozed down the bookshelves.

"God damn it!" Paul said. "I'm not trying to be your father, but this is my house! Clean that up!"

"Fuck you! You clean it up!" Chan kicked the chair in front of him, sending it over on its side, and headed for the door.

"Do not go out that door," Mamma ordered and then begged. "Chan, please, do not leave!"

Out of the door and into the night like clockwork. My mother cried and wiped the floor and table while yelling at Paul.

"He is the child! You are the adult! Can't you be nice? EVER?"

Paul turned to me and attempted to make sympathetic eye contact because I was the last one standing. I smiled but it was forced and fake. When he gave up and left the room Mamma turned her anger on me.

"Neither of you give Paul a chance. Chan's horrible but you are every bit as dismissive and rude as you can be!"

"I'm going to my room," I said in tears.

"Good."

I sat at my white desk and turned on the night-light of my vanity mirror wrapped with pink and yellow flowers and green iron vines. It was time. Time for the freedom unveiled when I climbed out of my window and into the night. It was time to breathe, time for my high school friends to pick me up, give me cigarettes and bourbon and meet the cute boys outside of their dark houses. I curled my hair and put in feather roach-clip combs, applied bubblegum lip-gloss and blue eye shadow, stared out the window and waited for my ride.

Fifteen

"You are the woman that I've always dreamed of…"

FIREFLY

Kentucky 1979

It was his sophomore year when Chan decided to move back to Kentucky and live with Mammy and Pappy on Elm Street in Versailles. He was trying to retrace his steps and get back what was lost. He wanted to go to high school at Sayre, the private school we attended in elementary. Chan felt deeply that this was where we belonged and he was going to stick to that plan come Hell or high water.

He moved into the Cabin. He was in his element, with the security blanket of our grandparents and cousins back in place. Chan was confident there like nowhere else. Our cousins were like his brothers, Ben was two years older, Whit one year younger and Matthew three years younger. He drove the windy old roads that he knew like the back of his hand. He played basketball and again became an instant celebrity. The coach said he had never seen such natural talent.

"Chan always talked about how much he hated Texas, absolutely despised it." Whit said. "He was excited to be back but scared

85

at the same time. Chan was the most well-known and popular person there, hands down. Everyone wanted to know him."

"Everything I did, Chan would say, 'That is so cool!'" Whit remembered his cousin playing fairy Godmother, "and everything I said, he would laugh and go, 'You are so funny man!' He was taking care of his little brother. Making sure I got pulled up the social ladder."

"When he first moved back here, he was going through a disco phase," Whit continued. "He had all these disco clothes, the feathered hair and these big ridiculous shoes with enormous heels. I think he had just seen *Saturday Night Fever* and *Grease*, and he was constantly doing all these disco moves. Ben gave him unshirted hell about it," he chuckled. "He teased him so much he finally dropped the whole thing by Christmas."

"Leader came to visit that first year. Nobody at Sayre knew what to make of him," Whit laughed. "I remember the two of them passed out hundreds of those Caesar's gold medallions from your dad. Every kid in school had a big gold medallion around their neck. It was hysterical."

It was fall of that same year when I came back to Kentucky to visit Chan. I was in the eighth grade. I followed him around and he showed me his world… our world.

He took me around my old school. I hadn't been there since the fourth grade and I had never been on the high school side of the campus. The softly lit mahogany hallways carried a sense of royalty and privilege. All the students had uniforms. The girls wore white button-down blouses, with blue and gray plaid skirts. The guys wore khaki pants and white shirts, with a mandatory blazer and tie.

I felt exposed and even sexy for the first time in my silk caramel-colored shirt and zip-up jeans. I had been in Texas for two years now, and I felt different. I was vulnerable and shy as we went from classroom to classroom. Chan was so comfortable he seemed like the principal. He had a swagger that was a little Mick Jagger, a little Dean Martin and totally original.

"Chan, where are you supposed to be?" a teacher said popping his head out of a classroom.

"My baby sister's in town, I gotta show her around!" he said with his head cocked back, a big smile across his face. The teacher smirked and ducked back in his room.

Chan proudly put his arm around me as we walked around the school. The leaves were changing and the wind was blowing. The air was crisp and fresh as we walked by red brick buildings covered with ivy. I felt at home, but so far away.

John Schremly appeared leaning against the doorframe at the cabin, smoking a joint. "Hey Guy."

John had pale skin, dark hair, and rosy cheeks, the same handsome Irish looks of Chan's other friend Todd O'Neill, who passed him a bottle of Wild Turkey. All three were in similar scruffy uniforms. Their navy sports coats hung open, shirts untucked and ties loosened. They all had the same casual arrogance of a very elite world, like they knew the answers to everything.

I fell quiet in this more sophisticated environment and followed Chan's lead. I thought that I should be going to Sayre and being treated delicately. I should be going to the country club, wearing skirts and pearls like my mom had. I felt like I belonged, but also a little damaged. Chan and I smiled at each other, a hidden understanding behind our eyes. This is who we would have been if things hadn't taken such a drastic turn.

Sixteen

"Dirty deeds, done dirt cheap…"

AC/DC

Lubbock, Texas 1980

In a pair of white painter's pants, a T-shirt and high-top tennis shoes, I met my friends at Gary Nazareneth's house to take acid for the first time. I was fifteen. Karen, Kelly and Kimber were three of the wildest girls in school, so consequently they became my best friends. We all wore red bandanas on our heads to comfort us through our 'trip.'

Sitting in Gary's ranch-style kitchen on his parent's peach, Formica countertop, we drank loads of some concoction akin to White Lightning. When we were good and juiced up, it was time to drop our designated blotter hits of Donald Duck acid. The next thing I knew, I was sitting on the floor of one of the bedrooms, spellbound in front of a painting of an ocean. Wide eyed, I watched the sea roll in and out, in and out, in and out. The luminescent seagull at the top of the painting swooped slowly down and dipped into the water. The water splashed and I watched the bird as it flew back up. It was a trick painting, I was sure of it. More than a trick, maybe it was actually magic. When I returned one pale and dusty summer afternoon to poke my head in the empty bedroom with a shag carpet and shoddy, crooked painting of a sea on the wall, a sea that did not move at all, I got the picture.

That school year, I sniffed Rush, amyl nitrate in a little brown bottle, in French class. During lunch hour, I crossed the street with my friends and we got drunk at the Mexican restaurant before returning to school, wild and wobbly. We sat in the backseat of a Trans Am and snorted some horrendous stinging substance called 'crank.' I stuffed four girls in the hatch back of my Mazda RX7, Chan bought with his black jack winnings at seventeen, and we drove along the wide, flat, brown streets screaming like banshees, *"Dirty deeds… done dirt cheap!"*

Lubbock was a dry town. I was usually the appointed driver to go to the strip and buy alcohol with our fake IDs. We got large Cokes and poured out half, filling the other half with Jack Daniels. Then we drove up 72nd Street to Taco Bell, the place to be. There, we pulled up next to the other cars in the parking lot and spent the evening dancing and singing and stumbling over to the boys we had crushes on. Then we made out with them. That was the social scene of the dusty plains.

Erin and Kimber Eschle, Lubbock, Texas

Around midnight it was time to sober up and go home, which meant it was time for me to air out. I was so paranoid and everyone made fun of me because I went through an intense ritual with the windows down and my hands and head hanging outside. I chewed mounds of gum, ate handfuls of mints then got out of the car and rolled in the grass saying, "air out! Air out! Air out!" All of this so I could walk into my house, cross the living room into my Mom's room and give her a kiss goodnight. Then go back to my room, shut my door and get into bed, get back up, go into the bathroom and throw up. Ahhh... what a night!

One evening Mamma came into my room and caught me dipping. I sat on my flowery quilt with a spit cup and a can of Skoal in my mouth. My head spinning like never before, I smiled. My mom was dumb struck. The same way she was horrified when I tried to leave for school in a tiny black top, skintight black Levi's, and cowboy boots. This was not how they dressed at the Idle Hour Country Club. What was happening to her little girl?

At the Monterey High School talent show Karen, Kelly, Kimber and I wore pink, white and baby blue terrycloth jump suits. I had combs clipping up the sides of my enormous perm and kinky bangs hanging down in front. I smiled from ear to ear with a mouth full of braces and danced to Heart's *"Kick it out! / Oh yeah, kick it out! / Come on, come on/ Kick out your motor and drive while you're still alive/ Kick it out!"*

Of course, I couldn't have gotten out of that Godforsaken place without losing my virginity. I was deeply infatuated with Craig the entire three years of high school. He was the cutest boy around, tall and tan and thin with a flashy white smile. He wore a cowboy hat over his thick black hair and had a slow and easy walk. Our flirtations began at the Taco Bell and various parties throughout the year but the climax came one week before my sixteenth birthday.

I had already decided after many notes passed, to let the inevitable take place. On the big night, my friend Kimber stayed over and we waited for my mom to go to sleep. When the house was completely silent, we nervously curled our hair and put on our lipgloss and eye shadow, inched across the hall and tiptoed down the stairs. In slow motion we turned the lock and slipped out the front door. The cool breeze of freedom was already upon us when we put my car in neutral and pushed it halfway down the block before turning it on and driving over to Byron's.

Byron was in the middle of his own sneaky routine when he met us at the door and put his finger up to his mouth. He was barefoot and motioned for us to take our shoes off. Then we crept back to Byron's bedroom. Craig was waiting and within an hour we were kissing in a sleeping bag on the floor.

"I love you," he whispered.

We had sex right there on the ground a few feet away from Kimber and Byron who pretended to sleep. It was more intimate than I ever would have dreamed. Tears streamed down my cheeks and I shook. He gently kissed my forehead, my eyes and my lips. We fell asleep in each other's arms. A few hours later, Kimber and I snuck back out into the night and back inside my house.

He didn't talk to me in the halls the next day. In fact we didn't talk at all until we were having sex again a few weeks later. I can't remember how I dealt with my sixteen-year-old heartache or how my little head full of braces dealt with Craig in the midst of his rejection, but I do remember that he started going steady with someone else. Her name was Carey I think. She was tall and thin with thick brown hair too so they made an extraordinarily beautiful, tan, athletic and popular couple. Even though I don't remember much, I'm sure that this quietly demoralizing experience set into motion decades of insecurity.

Still, I carried a torch for Craig until I was finally out of high school and out of that town. Then, like a cloud of smoke, it became like a dream. All those feelings went away and I had almost no opinion about Craig or anybody in Lubbock, good or bad. It was so clear that I was just passing through. I would join in and play in their crazy, dusty world, but I was just a visitor.

I almost missed my graduation. Karen and I were at some strange guy's studio apartment getting stoned. I remember he gave acid to his cat. He was really quite horrifying. We were there until minutes before getting our diplomas. Then we rushed out into the bright sun, threw on our powder blue graduation outfits and walked up the aisle. I just remember hoping my cap wouldn't fall off and thanking God I was getting out of there. I haven't been back since.

Seventeen

"This world, one more, then come the fireworks..."

MILDRED WATKINS CHANDLER

Kentucky 1983

W hen Mamma and Paul drove me across the country for college, I had the strangest sensation of loneliness and nervousness. They were taking me back *home*. I hadn't felt so scared
since I was little. As we crept further away from Texas and closer to
Kentucky, I had an overwhelming pit in my stomach. I had sort of
a breakdown somewhere on the road, in between the two worlds.
I felt incredibly hollow. I didn't know who I was anymore or who I
was about to be. I was going home but it felt really lonely.

Chan was in rare form around this point. He was living in an
apartment at the Merrick Inn in Lexington, which he eventually
burned down. He had been cooking out on the balcony and poured
hot coals in the trashcan before going for a drive. He arrived back
a few hours later to find fire trucks everywhere with his apartment
and everything in it destroyed.

You could rarely find Chan without a Heineken in his hand.
After gulping one down in his gold BMW, he had a nasty habit
of smashing it out the window at the feet of anyone unfortunate

enough to be passing by. Then he would raise both fists and strike a victory pose, grinning from ear to ear. Riding in a car with Chan was not something anyone with a high regard for mortality would ever want to do. He sped around hairpin curves at 90 miles an hour. You might have thought you were heading out to the country but could soon find that Chan had crossed the state lines and you were off on an adventure of his choice.

I moved in with Chan, into an apartment close to campus. We were both going to the University of Kentucky. It was the first time Chan and I had lived together since he left Texas. I was so excited to be with my big brother and bask in his familial protectiveness. We developed a weekend routine, driving from Lexington to Mammy's house in Versailles to do our laundry. We walked up the street to our old house at 156 Elm and dreamt about buying it back some day. We would swim in the pool beside the cabin and lay in the sun, waiting for Josephine to finish the daily feast of fried chicken, mashed potatoes and greens.

About a month into our cohabitation, we were running out the door around 11:00 in the morning. There was always a bong on the table with pot around. I had managed to sneak a few hits here and there but had never actually smoked in front of Chan. He told me when I got to Kentucky that if I wanted to smoke pot I had to do it with him. I wasn't allowed to smoke outside the house. We were off to lunch and just before I got to the door I decided to mosey over and take a bong hit.

"Jesus, Erie, what are you doing?" He asked incredulously.

"Just taking a hit." I said innocently.

"God Damnit! God Damnit!" He screamed. "What the fuck is wrong with you, it's 11:00 in the fucking morning! What do you need pot for at 11:00 in the morning?"

"I don't know, I just thought it would be fun." I said.

He threw his keys across the room and stormed back into the apartment. He started yelling about how he couldn't believe how I had turned out. He kicked a hole in the wall and went and got the tequila out of the refrigerator and began taking shots right out of the bottle. He sat on the floor, shook his head and started crying.

"You're just like me," he cried. "You're just fucking like me."

I felt sad and guilty for being the way I was. I was also worried that he was so out of control and out of proportion. I had always longed for Chan's courage and confidence, his absolute freedom but I also knew my brother was extremely troubled. We rallied as we always did and that terrible day turned into a normal night.

Chan wanted so badly for me to get off on the right foot now that I was back in Kentucky. He went so far as to insist that I be a debutante that season and had Mammy arrange the whole thing. This was a tradition many from Sayre followed so while beginning my first year in college and returning to my hometown, I was to be 'presented' to Lexington's high society. More to the point, I was to be re-presented to our childhood friends and their parents.

The night of the ball, of 'coming out,' I stood with eleven girls, all in our white gowns and long white gloves. I smiled demurely backstage, standing tall and elegant, waiting for my name to be called. Chan and Whit, looking dashing in their black tuxes and red sashes, were my escorts. Everyone in the ballroom silently and collectively agreed to play this scene right out of the fifties.

Chan, Dan and Whitney Chandler, Lexington, Kentucky

When my name came booming from the loudspeaker, Chan and Whit each took an arm and ceremoniously walked me to the edge of the stage where I curtsied to the ballroom of familiar faces. Some I remembered, most remembered me, and everyone knew someone from my family. They were all there, both sets of grandparents, aunts, uncles and cousins. It was a wonderful evening. I was strangely comfortable with the whole scene. This long white get-up suited me so much better than the feather earrings and tacky black tops of my Texas days, way back last month.

Erin, bottom row, far left, Debutante Ball, Lexington, Kentucky

That night was the beginning of many other nights like it. The summer was filled with ladies luncheons and lots of beautiful clothes. There was black-tie event after black-tie event at hotels in the city and grand southern mansions in the country. They all began with a lovely dinner with well thought out seating plans, then came dancing to an orchestra and DJ, finally we were escorted into another room for an elaborate breakfast at two in the morning to sober up.

I hadn't seen most of the people there since the fourth grade but they welcomed me as if I had been away for the summer. I certainly understood why Chan preferred this to the anonymous treatment we got in Texas. We had to make our own way in Lubbock. For us, thanks to our grandfather, in Kentucky the way was paved. Every door swung open.

Eighteen

*"Oh my love for the first time in my
life, my mind is wide open..."*

JOHN LENNON

Kentucky 1984

Pope McLean and I started dating that summer. His family lived in a beautiful white house on a sprawling horse farm. I struggle to explain how secure I felt there, but never quite like I belonged. I did know I had found a little piece of heaven. I loved standing on the fences, looking out over the countryside with the fresh breeze blowing through my hair. I loved hanging out in the barns with their horses.

It was all so wholesome. I felt I was me again. I was home again. As the Cure say, I was *clean again*. The nightmare of Texas, and that entire struggle was over. I was safe. Pope's family was calm and sweet and lovely, a far cry from the whirlwind of my crew. They had dinners every night together and kidded each other about things they did that day. My family had dinners together too but while the conversation was interesting, there was always someone in the midst of a nervous breakdown.

Pope's group just seemed to have it together. The land, the horses, the fresh air and the clean cut, beautiful family seemed to be enough to close the day with a smile. I often spent the night in his sister, Grandison's room. Next to that angelic little girl in the other twin bed, I experienced a few moments of what it would have been like to live in a truly stable home. One evening we all went out to a field at two in the morning to watch a horse give birth. Under a giant, warm spotlight, Pope and his Dad gently brought a beautiful foal into the world. I wanted to curl up in that big white house and sleep for a century.

I wore feminine summer dresses and hung out on the screened-in porch reading and drinking sweet tea. We took long drives in the country and went to the horse races and afternoon tailgate parties. We mingled on the polo grounds where girls sipped cocktails in dresses and pearls and boys drank Bourbon in khakis and loafers. Weekend nights, Pope put on his tux and I got dolled up and we went to debutante parties.

Pope came with me out west to see how the other half lived... loosely and wildly. In Lake Tahoe, my dad's new girlfriend Janet ran around in a T-shirt and underwear, tanned legs and hair dyed platinum blonde. We drove around the lake with Daddy, blaring music as happy tears poured out of his eyes. With the glorious mountains surrounding us, my father's main concern was that we understood every word Jimmy Buffett or Billy Joel sang.

Pope later came with me to Texas. There he witnessed my mom's calm and serene environment of books, soft music and glass mobiles hanging in the window catching the sunlight. He also got a heaping helping of my stepfather's war tales and stories of his pet tarantula and boa constrictor. Paul warned us about tapeworms and scurvy all the while checking me from the side of his eye with a suspicious grin on his face. He expected me to make fun of him, which I never did. I was always scared of him and tried to make him feel good and think that we were interested. It was uncomfortable. My little family unit was filled with love but screwed up and disjointed, nevertheless. It was the polar opposite of Pope's steadfast and grounded group.

We dated for four or five years and were really in love. For a time it was rare and beautiful and pure. Time stopped, no one else was in the universe. We were absolutely crazy for each other. Pope was the first person who loved me for exactly who I was. I felt like myself for the first time in a long time. We talked about getting married and having babies. He always said he couldn't wait to see me pregnant. I was "the most beautiful princess in the world." He sent me boxes of love letters and tapes and even cut out hearts in all shapes and sizes.

It was wonderful but we were so young. To make a long, sweet love story short, as we got older, he became more conservative and I became more curious. I was beginning to get excited about the possibility of living the life of an actress. Just as he decided his fate was on the farm, I decided I needed to experience the titillating world of the stage I had witnessed as a kid in Las Vegas. I wanted to feel the drums in my stomach again, the thrill of the curtain going up and the freedom of living a life outside of the norm.

I majored in Theatre at the University and quickly realized that Theatre people were my kind of people. I knew that was where I belonged. When I played Elizabeth in *Laundry and Bourbon*, everyone came backstage and hugged me. Chan had tears in his eyes and looked as if he were seeing me for the first time, "Erie, you were so amazing!"

Pope came up behind him and said casually, "I didn't get here until eight-fifteen. I almost missed it."

We were going our separate ways. We didn't get each other anymore. It took a long while after that to completely let go of one another. It was extremely hard to relinquish something that had been so intense. I started drinking heavily and acting like a lunatic, daring to drive him away and eventually I did.

"I don't want my wife to be an alcoholic!" Pope once said.

"That's gonna' be somebody else's problem," I replied, chock full of arrogance and ignorance.

When we finally let go, it was like saying goodbye to the only stable family I had ever known. Suddenly, there was no one to watch over me, no one to take care of me, no one to keep me grounded. The balloon cord was cut and I was floating again, alone and not too good at taking care of myself.

I remember seeing him with his new girlfriend, about a month after we broke up, a little blonde sorority girl was in the passenger seat of his BMW... my seat. Her head was bobbing and she was smiling as they drove past my house. I ran into the kitchen sobbing, physically nauseous.

My dad loved Pope but of course took my side over anyone. Daddy had his own way of dealing with such things. He sent me some money and told me to have a champagne party. I took his advice and filled the refrigerator of my little Woodland Avenue apartment with Dom Perignon, had a party and moved on.

He married that same little blonde from the car that day. I went on to have several romances. I had the mandatory and cliché two-year love affair with a very handsome Italian name Piero, whom I met while studying theatre at Kings College in England. It was like a movie. We had picnics in the park. We went to see plays and popped in little romantic cafés. My hair was long and curly. I wore ballet flats and pretty flowered dresses that matched the lavish gardens of London.

Then came a just as mandatory and cliché three years of torment with a writer in Los Angeles. That was like a movie too, but more like a horror film. It didn't start out that way but ended in my near self-destruction. I can't even bring myself to say his name, but it was just as ordinary and anti-climactic as the whole affair turned out to be. There were a few others interspersed but it wasn't until I met Samuel, that I felt the same unconditional love as with Pope. It was a long, lonely road between the two but it was worth the wait to experience true love again, something so easy and natural and light.

Nineteen

"Nobody knows you, when you're down and out. In your pocket, not one penny, and as for friends, you don't have any..."

JIMMIE COX

Kentucky February 2003

"**N**o man is a match for a designing woman!" Daddy announced.

My blank gaze drifted from the conspicuously empty swimming pool over to my father and back again. We had been in the Cabin for one month and Sam and I had consented to our new roles. Assigned by Daddy, I was cast as the whimsical idiot, Sam was the fixer upper, and he was the Buddha on the mountaintop. My dad appointed himself as the all-knowing sage and made sure we caught every pearl of wisdom he dropped from his bedroom to the kitchen, out to the porch and back through the living room. It was a sort of twisted *All In The Family*, I was Gloria, just an alcoholic one, Sam was the perfect Meathead and Daddy was of course, Archie.

Erin Chandler

"In other words," he took a sip of scotch, "You take a female that is a designing person, a person that is designing in any way and she is a big favorite over any male."

"What do you mean a designing person?" I looked up from my burning cigarette and attempted to engage, to politely receive the lesson being delivered.

"A person with ulterior motives!" he snapped, eyes bulging and accusing me of ignorant naiveté. "A person that's trying to slip up on somebody's blind side to manipulate them for any reason, and you know there are girls... Hey! Monica Lewis!" He screamed, mispronouncing the notorious intern's name. "She grabbed the President's too too and he followed her right down."

"Adam!" He yelled again, happy to find dumbass-male-number-two. "Eve showed him an apple and said, 'Here, take a bite.'"

My mind was exhausted from weeks of metaphors and loosely disguised insults. I glared at him and he glared back. He didn't take a puff of his cigar or a sip of his Scotch. It was a Mexican standoff.

"Is there somethin' in there that makes sense to you?" He broke the silence, squinting angrily. "Is there a lesson somewhere in there for you?"

"Yeah." I raised my eyebrows and shrugged.

"Then laminate it!!" he demanded.

And so went our days and nights until nature took center stage. One particularly bitter cold, snowy eve, Daddy, Sam and I were sharing the giant Moroccan couch, watching a documentary about Michael Jackson. Suddenly, the power went out, catapulting us into silent darkness.

Knowing the Cabin would get cold quickly, we decided to go directly to sleep. Lit candles showed us the way back to our bedrooms and we rushed to savor what warmth had accumulated. Still under the assumption that the power would kick back on in a few hours, we were blissfully unaware that it was the cusp of one of the worst ice storms in Kentucky history.

The light of dawn woke me up and my nose was frozen. I covered my entire head, burying my face under Sam's warm arm.

"It didn't come back on," he said, half asleep.

"We're living inside a refrigerator," I said from under the covers.

"Erin Lynne!" Daddy called out." Come look at this!"

Sam rolled over and took his arm away exposing me to the frigid air. I pulled a freezing sweatshirt over my pajamas and walked into the igloo the Cabin's living room had become. Daddy was standing in front of the wide-open front door in his boxer shorts. Beyond my father I saw an iced fairyland. Three inches of cloudless, frozen water covered the tree branches. Long, clear, spear-like icicles hung from every solid surface. In spite of the bitter cold it was exciting and beautiful.

I hugged Daddy while we took in the extraordinary scene. Nature had prevailed and brought with it silence and splendor. An apocalypse of pure white blanketed our old ideas under a renewed clear, blue sky. Every lawn up and down Elm Street was littered with iced branches. Trunks of giant Oaks were uprooted. Power lines were torn down and hanging between trees, covered with still more limbs and more ice. Versailles was asleep below the weight of this glistening universe.

"That is the height of spoiled!" Daddy lit a cigar and yelled into his cell phone at his friends who rushed to the Hyatt and Marriott Hotels. Every room in Lexington was booked within a day but my father, still in his boxers and t-shirt, pitied those sucked into the panic.

It became apparent quickly that we were going to ride this out so Sam built a blazing fire and I pushed the couch and plushy chairs right up against the giant stone fireplace. It was romantic, the three of us all bundled up and trapped in together. The fire was our only source of heat in the sub-zero weather. We could even leave milk on the kitchen counter and it stayed ice cold.

Sam kept that fire going all day and all night. We slept on the couch inches from the flame and wore layers of clothing, only peeling off the essential layer when we had to. And when we absolutely had to, we stepped away from the fireplace and ran into the freezing part of the Cabin and onto the blocks of ice the toilets had become. Then we sprinted back into the cavernous living room and back in front of the fire. Thus resuming what was beginning to feel like a 60's love-in.

"Want to hear it? Here it goes…" Sam said, guitar in hand, jumping into a rousing rendition of *"Nobody Knows You When You're Down and Out"* and *"Is You Is or Is You Ain't My baby?"*

With the usual white noise of the television, the numbing cacophony of news and sports gone, we went into a time warp. The only thing left was conversation and candlelight. I had been craving a respite from the constant striving and planning and figuring, a break from life as I knew it. I got my wish with Daddy and Sam at my side. There was nowhere to go, no one to be. I should have joined a circus or a band. With the personality of a carny or a roadie, I come by it naturally. My uncle always called my grandmother, *a road show*. I too am happiest when every moment is all for one and one for all. I got that feeling again in front of the everchanging flames as Daddy fired away anecdotes and Sam played blues songs. Like a good prairie woman, I put soup in a cast iron kettle over the fire.

'Crackle, crackle, boom!' we heard at regular intervals. Branches fell hard from the weight of the ice. I panicked when Sam went outside, which he constantly did in order to get more wood.

There were loose wires hanging everywhere and I was scared that he would get electrocuted. The town was in a state of emergency and that was reinforced with every ill constructed sentence coming through the airwaves.

"I'm tellin' yeeewww," came a voice from the small radio hooking us up to the surrounding hillbilly world. "No 'lectric, neighbors got no 'lectric neither. Hadn't had in three days. Wife put one a' them generators inside. Damn near blew up the place!"

Freddy Siegelman, the mayor of Versailles, came by to check on us and listen to Daddy's latest tale. When we eventually ran out of wood, Freddy brought us old railroad ties to burn.

On day three of the blackout, my cousin Ben burst through the door. "Anybody alive in here? Uncle Dan?"

We looked toward the beacon of light at the other end of the room, the sun and bright snow served as a halo around Ben in the doorway. Deliriously, we ran over to welcome him into our frozen world. He brought us a huge banquet of Kentucky Fried Chicken from Frankfort, the only city nearby with power.

"I bet you guys are hungry!"

"Ohhh Hooo Man!" Daddy exclaimed. "I can't tell you how good this looks!"

Standing in the kitchen in our scarves and hats we devoured a feast that tasted as good as any Thanksgiving. Like savages we grinned and dipped hunks of chicken into mashed potatoes and gravy, stuffing the savory warmth into our mouths.

After five long days and nights, we surrendered and drove an hour to Louisville for a hotel room. The three of us looked like hell, we were so emotionally rung out. Thawing for the first time in a week was a slow and sensitive process. Sam, Daddy and I literally couldn't speak as we gently let go of muscles that had been tensed up for days.

Our first stop out of Versailles was the IHOP. The soothing coffee shop nearly sent us into sobs. Leaning over our eggs like Neanderthals in parkas and boots, we gradually melted. Then, like defeated players after a hard game, we limped back to the car, drove to the nearest hotel and collapsed.

For the next three days we anxiously awaited news that the 'lectric was back on and it was safe to return home. While it was wonderful to lie in a warm, cozy bed and watch TV, this situation had its own challenges. Daddy talked as loudly in his sleep as he did awake. Sam slept through night after night with Tylenol PM and earplugs. I lay awake listening in deafening volumes but crystal clear sentences, Daddy introduced the University of Kentucky basketball coach, "Tubby Smith everyone!!! Here he is!! Introducing Tubby Smith!"

Another night Daddy explained a football jersey to a dream friend, very impressed with the handiwork, "It was done amazingly, real intricate."

Finally, Freddy called to report the coast was clear and we drove back to Versailles. Daddy slept in the backseat, his head resting on his chest, cigar dangling from his mouth like a big baby. We stepped into the dark, cavernous Cabin and flipped the switch. Miraculously, the place was illuminated. Within minutes, my father was back at his desk making phone calls and I was opening a bottle of red and preparing a meatloaf. The train was back on track like nothing had ever happened.

Twenty

"Somebody said they saw me, swinging the world by the tail, bouncing over a white cloud, killing the blues..."

ALISON KRAUSS

Kentucky March 2003

"It was almost like Chan was reveling in the shock value," Pope settled in between Sam and me on the big Moroccan couch. "I don't know. Maybe that wasn't the reason, but he was trying to be sensational with it all."

I had invited my old boyfriend over to the Cabin because I needed an ally. I wanted to be with someone who knew me before I stammered my sentences, before I was afraid of everything. When I told Daddy to get dressed because Pope was coming over, he shook his head and walked back to his bedroom, "I don't know why you're doing this."

He acted like I was determined to screw everything up. I certainly was not. I only wanted proof of the drama I had been through, maybe then I could make sense of all the nervousness. I wanted an eyewitness for my post-traumatic stress disorder.

"Another gun incident I remember," Pope continued, "because he always had guns. You all had some little plot of land around here in Versailles and some guys were on there and he just unloaded at their feet! Yelling at them, telling them to get off. And the local Barney's, the sheriffs, were not happy. One of the bullets shot into somebody's house!" He laughed.

"Want another beer?" I placed a plate of cheese and crackers in front of him.

"Sure. I remember he was sober for a year or two, I don't remember. But I ran into him at Copperfield's and he told me, 'I'm gonna start drinking again.' And I said 'Chan, why would you do that? You're such a nice guy when you're sober.' And I'm telling this to his face! 'And when you drink, you're such an asshole! Why? Why would you do that?' He just shrugged. No answer." Pope put his head down. "I've never met anybody like him, never will. He went to the extreme."

I hadn't talked to Pope in years, but there was something about being in the Cabin, struggling with Sam financially and emotionally that made me long for that non-judgmental security I felt with Pope.

"That room upstairs was Chan's lair," Pope said, pointing upstairs to the room above us, overlooking the pool, the devil room I called it. "I remember your grandfather was always trying to get him out. It would have taken a stick of dynamite to get him out of there," he laughed.

Daddy came in and gave Pope a big cigar and put his arm around Sam. Then he looked down at my drink. "Is that Coke?"

"Coke with a splash of something a little more exciting," I smiled.

"The guy had a huge heart," Pope went on. "He was so generous, if he liked you he would do anything for you but if he didn't, well, let's just say he'd let you know." He shook his head and took a sip of beer, "He certainly had a strong personality. He always asserted himself."

"Did he ever," Pat Wilhoit walked in and eased into the conversation. "I remember I was like twenty when Chan took me to the Chicken Ranch, the whorehouse outside Vegas. We only had like two hundred dollars between us. I remember they had a big piano and Chan knew I played so he made me perform in front of like thirty prostitutes! The only thing I could think of to play was *Imagine*. All the prostitutes were singing and Chan was singing along and laughing. Then I guess he negotiated for two of them and we... you know... and that was that." Pat laughed. "He was taking care of his little brother."

Pat lit a Marlboro Light and moved his body around in his chair. He had adopted some of Chan's mannerisms. Fluid, like a dancer, his head was held up high and he had a groovy sort of self-effacing giggle that was both confident and filled with humility.

"I remember in 1987 he took me to the World Series," Pat went on. "The Minnesota Twins were playing the Cardinals in St. Louis. Your dad got us tickets and we had breakfast with Tommy Lasorda, the manager of the Los Angeles Dodgers. Chan went up to him and Mr. Lasorda gave him a big hug and said, 'Hey! How is your grandfather?' and all that. I must have been eighteen when he took me the first time, he'd come and sign me out of school, I don't know if he was going to college then or not."

"I'm guessing not," I said. "Chan slipped in and out of college for years. He went to UK and Santa Monica College and I think UNLV for a minute. At some point he gave up the whole idea of finishing."

"Oh man, I told you about that Bulls game in Chicago, didn't I?" Pat asked me. "Chan had tickets for the Championship Finals. We were walking in broad daylight, about two in the afternoon and when we reached the lake there were thousands of people around and Chan starts taking his clothes off! Just stripped down! This big crowd is just looking on in shock. He handed me his clothes and did a swan dive into Lake Michigan, buck-naked. People on the bridge and in the boats were pointing and freaking out." Pat shrugged his shoulders and took a drag. "Then he swam to the side and I met him at the shore, handed him his clothes and he got dressed. That was that. It was just an impulse thing,"

Sam excused himself and went upstairs. He didn't get the humor in it, didn't understand how we could sit around and laugh about something so audacious. It was completely foreign to him.

"Then after the game we drove straight through to Vegas," Pat continued, barely noticing Sam's departure, "drove thirty hours straight to Vegas."

"What did you all do in Las Vegas?" I asked.

Laura Gross, Willie Nelson, Chan Chandler and friend, Las Vegas

"Ohh hooo," he leaned back in his chair. "We hung out with Leader, which was... shooo... boy that was something. Everyday in the morning we would get up and go down to the Sports Book. It was really close to your dad's place down there by the Hilton, and we would go hang out with this guy named Paul, I never knew who he was. Then one day I was watching ESPN and it was Paul Hornung! One of the greatest football players of all time and we'd been hanging out with him every day!"

"He was one of Daddy's best friends," I said. Daddy's best friends were always legendary players and coaches, always super-stars of their chosen field, sports, law or organized crime.

"I think at that time Chan was trying to get supporters, you know, contributors to help Ben. I think this must have been the second time I went to Vegas, because your cousin Ben was running for auditor or something, I think Chan was sober that second time. Wow, it's so cloudy. But like I said we'd spend the day hanging out at the Sports Book and then we'd go out at night. Leader would have like fifty thousand dollars in one pocket and the other pocket was just full of pills! They weren't even in anything, just in his pocket! And he would just pull out a handful and say, 'Here, you want some, Patrick?'"

"What were they?" I asked.

"Oh, Xanax, Valium, Percocet... you know, anything. I'd pick out a couple of Xanax. I'll never forget, we went out to dinner with these kinda shady... I think they were from El Paso... friends of your dad's. I had just gotten my hair cut and I was fucked up on those pills. This man said, 'you look like an idiot,' or something, 'you look like a poster boy for Super Cuts', or something. And I was like 'Fuck you, I'll kill you!' Chan was like, 'wooooo, don't say that, this guy'll like have you buried' or whatever, you know? I didn't know!" Sweet sheltered Patrick, clueless that he was in the presence of honest to goodness bad guys.

"I'm trying to think if this was the same trip Chan blacked my eye out." Pat recalled more seriously, "We were walking somewhere in Vegas and he picked up some black lady, I guess it was a hooker, I don't know, and we went back to his place. I was on Xanax and passed out. He tried to wake me up because he couldn't get me off the bed. Next thing I know he stood me up, I saw his fist comin' and WHAM! He dotted my eye. He punched me right in the eye and I was, like, unconscious!" He laughed. Pat is a big guy and it was hard to picture him being picked up and punched.

"We ended up getting in a huge fight and the police came and took me to your dad's. It was in that apartment, you remember when Chan had that apartment it was kinda' down the street from your dad's? I don't know why you guys had it, but it was in the Las Vegas Country Club. Chan had it for just a little while, I don't know why he had it… it was just kinda' like a place to go. So the cops took me to your dad's and I went in there and got a tennis racket, and was walking back to the apartment. I was gonna, you know… I was delirious!" He giggled. "The cops picked me back up and said 'oh no.'"

"Did Chan get arrested?"

"No, they just let him go and the next day he was like mortified and he was crying, telling me how sorry he was, that I was his little brother and he would do anything for me. I guess I shouldn't have gotten that hammered." Pat lit another cigarette before getting up and strutting to the kitchen to get another beer, "I'm trying to think of another Vegas story, but mainly I was just scared half the time!"

"Remember that Vern poster?" Pope sat straight up. "Remember we were sitting there one night in that little apartment he had in Lexington? All of a sudden our ears were ringing. Chan had shot… there was that guy, the 'Hey Vern' guy… you know what I'm talking about? And boom!" he yelled. "He shot him right through the forehead. And we were like, 'What the… what the hell did you just do?' And he gets up and looks through the peephole of the front door, you know, thinking, 'Oh shit, what the hell did I just do? I shouldn't have done that!'" Pope was witness to a lot of Chan' scandalous behavior but this was a little too close for comfort. "He got up and looked through the peephole to see if anybody was coming. You just sat there in shock."

"I was in shock!" I said.

"I remember I went back a day later, that bullet had gone through two walls and wedged into a two by four in the closet. I remember taking a knife and sure enough, I dug the slug out."

"It's crazy," I said.

"Oh yeah, it's crazy. He could have killed somebody." Pope leaned back on the couch. Then defended Chan, "but he wasn't trying to hurt anybody."

"See! See?" I pleaded with them. "It's insane! And it was always like that. No wonder I'm petrified of guns and so skittish! It's just… it's just insane!"

I was trying to intellectualize it, trying to get past it, trying to figure out why I felt so messed up all the time. Why I was so petrified of guns. Why every time I walked by a cop I prayed for control, sure I would grab his gun and shoot someone or myself. I couldn't bear the proximity to such a deadly circumstance. All that was between death and me was two inches and whatever self-control I could muster. If I lost either, I was a goner, either in jail for the rest of my life trying to explain those two seconds, or dead. It was too much responsibility. I feel the same way when I'm by a bridge or a tall building. I'm always shocked that some hotels or apartment buildings have these balconies twenty and fifty stories up with just a flimsy rail. They leave it to the common sense of the masses not to get too close. I, for one, want a little more protection between my wiry brain and myself. I never want the possibility of extinction to be so close.

Sam and I once lived in a tiny apartment in Studio City, down the street from a flower shop that was next to a bridge over the freeway. Driving over that bridge I always felt like I might accidentally jump out of the car and climb right over! I knew I was being ridiculous so, one day, I thought 'face your fears' and decided to take a walk over that bridge.

It was three in the afternoon and there was massive traffic so everyone was driving very slowly. The bridge was only about half a block long, but the freeway was zooming below and the cement railing only came to my hip. I had a horrendous case of vertigo and I was sure I would fall or jump. I almost crouched down and crawled across. Instead, I chanted, "I'm okay, I'm okay, I'm okay, I'm okay," over and over again until I made it to solid ground. That was one of my top ten anxiety attacks. I had to walk several blocks up the street to a grocery store to call a cab so they would drive me back over the bridge. I fought my fears and my fears won.

I know this raises questions of sanity or maybe even a death wish but I think I'm actually the polar opposite of suicidal. I really want to be here. It just seems way too easy not to be. There is so much I want to do in this life. There are so many incredible things to discover and experiences to be had but I get so insanely neurotic at times, the future seems elusive. I believe this is because I lived my whole life with the person I loved the most, literally on the edge.

Malibu 1985

"Chan, please get down!" I cried.

Chan had jumped up on the railing of the pier outside Alice's restaurant. The railing was about three inches thick and my brother teetered unsteadily several stories above the crashing waves and rocky shore.

"Come on Chan, man," Pope said. "Get off of there."

*"Chan, get down! You are going to kill yourself! Get off of there!"
Lissa screamed.*

"gegegegegegegegegegegegegege" Chan mocked in a baby voice. He wiggled and writhed down the tightrope above the sea and stones with a Corona in his hand.

"I'm not watching this," I said and stormed off.

"Hey kid, where are you going?" Chan laughed.

Tears were pouring out of Lissa's eyes as she fled the scene.

Chan jumped down and followed after her, "Lissa relax, come here…"

Twenty-One

*"I'm just a mother of a man, I got the stopper in my
hand. Judge and jury help me please, ain't gonna
get down on my knees, God help me now..."*

MICK JAGGER

Kentucky February 2003

"Rehabs?" Daddy said, sitting in a rocking chair, the ever-present cigar dangling from his lips. "With Chan?"

"Weren't there seven?" I asked.

"At least. Jesus, that wore my ass out," he lowered his head, the wind was taken out of him just talking about it. "There was Hazelton, I know. That place up in Aspen, Betty Ford a couple times. Then Charter Ridge and a couple of those local places..."

"I remember the first one was the Betty Ford Center," his voice trailed off, deep in memory. "Your Mamma and I picked him up at some stranger's house. He was rail thin and I hugged him and he was trembling all over. We told him we were going to take him with us. On the flight, your Mamma begged the stewardess not to give him anything to drink, but she served him anyway and he was roaring drunk when we got there. Then they told us there would be a wait of two, maybe three weeks. Your Mamma almost had a breakdown, started sobbing and sobbing and the lady looked at her and said 'Don't you know that just because he's here, it doesn't mean he'll stay sober.' And she said, well he has to! We'd been through hell to get him there. She thought she couldn't live if he didn't stay. Little did we know that was the first of about 13 treatment centers."

Lynne and Chan, Aspen, Colorado

Chan wrote his own defense/twelfth step/confession/apology:

"Emotionally I have been either recuperating or an absolute wreck. My outlook on life is so sporadic that at times I feel like I can accomplish anything, that things are on the upswing, and that all my problems and fears and guilt are behind me. Then on the other hand I feel completely destitute, wondering what my future holds, if anything. In complete bewilderment about how strong I actually am, wondering whether I will absolutely lose everything, my mind, my family, and everything that means anything to me.

For the amount of alcohol and drug abuse that I have put my body through, I am surprised I'm able to function. I believe my major concern would have to stem from a highly serious intake of marijuana. I smoke every day several times a day (4-10 highs per day). I often find myself out of breath and cough regularly. I am concerned that I may be in some phase of emphysema, which scares me since I understand once you develop emphysema, it never gets any better than the stage it hits. Secondarily, my brain cells have been being massacred by whiskey, wine and beer. I'm sure I haven't progressed mentally much since I was about 18.

Alcohol and drugs have caused me endless problems with all my family members. It is a wonder I still have them. They have been used, neglected, and hurt for far too long. I love them dearly, but when I'm drinking or have been drinking, I curse, verbally abusing them, saying things to hurt them, telling them I hate them and constantly taking advantage of them. On one occasion, I slapped my baby sister for getting excited and begging me to stop abusing myself! I even gave her the impression I was too busy for her problems as I recently uncovered in a letter. My family means everything to me and this abuse has simply got to end.

I've broken nearly all of my personal values, taking pride in the fact that nothing is sacred, laughing at such solemn things as death, accidents and misfortune.

My social life has been enhanced by the use of alcohol and drugs. This is not to say that I haven't lost friends and girlfriends because of over-indulgence but for the most part I have relied heavily on drugs as a status symbol and alcohol to give me nerve to break the ice that once was ever present. Drugs have been a useful key for many of my relationships but on the other hand, I would have been much better off making true friends on my own rather than using the façade.

I don't think alcohol or drugs have affected my spirituality one way or the other. Although I certainly don't act very Christian towards my fellow man when I'm drinking, I do believe in God, and always have, as the creator and maker of all. But I have never been very church going or deeply religious.

Drugs and alcohol have played a part in my work as far as not having the incentive to work. I have definitely had the opportunity to become self-supporting and simply neglected it, deeming it easier to remain dependent on my folks and accept their generosity.

My school life has plummeted to hell as a result of my drugs and drinking. Once an honor roll student, I now have 48 hours in four years of college at a 2.14 standing, just .14 away from unsatisfactory grades at a state university. The fact that I failed my first class at the exact same year I started smoking grass is much more than coincidental. And the fact that I elected to take a G.E.D. rather than take a full load my senior year displays a true sense of weakness.

I have most certainly done things that no normal person would dream of. Punching walls until my fists were bloody and crippled, punching out windows, breaking things that were extremely valuable, such as stereos, televisions, windshields, furniture, etc. Firing guns in the city, and inside my house. Pointing loaded guns at people and myself just to get a reaction out of them. Challenging police officers' authority, cursing them and threatening them, time after time heading back to harmful substances such as cocaine, alcohol and Valium, even though I know I know quite well the perils of their abuse.

I have wrecked at least ten automobiles under the influence, three times I should have been killed. I have continued to fight even though I have had my nose broken twice and have been put in the hospital with ten stitches in my face alone. Putting myself in precarious positions while drinking has become commonplace. Using Cocaine intravenously, using Valium with large amounts of alcohol, drinking so much I would have to hang my head out the window to stay up and many things I am sure I have forgotten about."

My brother was sentenced to the Pitkin County jail in Aspen, Colorado for six months. I told him it didn't look like a jail to me. It looked like a college dorm. There were no bars, just doors and a nice seating area around a little kitchen. "I wouldn't want to stay in Caesar's Palace for six months!" Chan protested.

He sent me a card while he was there, a painting of a child that looked like him when he was six or seven. The little boy was sitting on a fence, looking over beautiful green rolling hills, the sun over his head. On the return address he wrote, 'Chan' and he boxed his name in with lines like bars around it.

Twenty-Two

"Man faces sentencing for
seventh D.U.I. In aspen"

Police Report: Aspen Colorado 1988
"The defendant was traveling from Vail to Aspen in his
BMW, hit another vehicle in a parking lot outside of
town, left the scene and proceeded into Aspen, where
he hit another vehicle. The operators of the BFI trash
disposal truck witnessed the first accident, followed
the defendant into town, witnessed the second accident and confronted the operator of the BMW about his
failure to report either accident. The defendant then
offered the operator of the BFI truck $100 if he would
not report the accident. When the police arrived on
the scene the defendant identified himself as Albert
Benjamin Chandler III. The officers observed the
smell of alcohol on Chandler's breath, slurred speech
and unsteadiness on his feet. He refused to perform
roadside tests and was arrested for D.U.I. and refused
a blood or Breathalyzer test. A container of prescription drugs, Xanax was found in the defendant's pocket
at the time of his arrest.

Defendant's statement:

Mr. Chandler gave a description of the incident compatible with the police reports during our interview. He stated that he was on his way home to Las Vegas from Vail, saw the highway sign to Aspen and decided to drive up valley. He was drinking vodka and grapefruit juice on the trip to Aspen and took a number of Xanax. He probably consumed a pint of vodka prior to his arrest.

The defendant does not recall being involved in any car accidents. He does not remember trying to bribe a witness but admits he may have attempted to pay for damages. He does admit that he gave his cousin's name when questioned by officers. He also used his cousin's name when booked into the Pitkin County Jail.

Prior Legal History:

1982 D.U.I.   Lexington, Kentucky
1982 D.U.I.   Lexington, Kentucky
1984 D.U.I   Versailles, Kentucky (pending wanton endangerment)
1984 D.U.I.   Las Vegas, Nevada
1987 D.U.I.   Lubbock, Texas (two years probation)
1987 D.U.I.   Lexington, Kentucky (one year probation)
1988 Unlawful Carrying of a Weapon Lubbock, Texas

Social Background:

Joseph Daniel Chandler Jr. is the older of two children born to Joseph Daniel and Lynne Chandler in Lexington, Kentucky. His parents divorced in 1973 when he was about ten years old. His mother remarried Paul Knipping, a professor at Texas Tech University in Lubbock, Texas. The defendant reports that his father was a stockbroker in Kentucky, went through bankruptcy, owned a tennis concession stand in Miami for a period and then moved to Las Vegas, where he is a casino host for Caesars Palace. The defendant enjoys a close relationship with his sister, who is a college student in Lexington, and with his paternal grandfather, who also resides in Kentucky.

Education:
Mr. Chandler attended high schools in Lexington and Versailles, Kentucky, in Lake Tahoe, Nevada and Lubbock, Texas. He states that he received his G.E.D. in 1981 and attended the University of Kentucky in Lexington for two years. He referred to his occupation as "student" and stated that he intended to return to school as soon as this legal matter is cleared up.

Employment:
This 25- year-old defendant reports three periods of employment. For one week in May of 1988 Joseph served as a Kentucky Derby consultant for Harrah's of Atlantic City. He arranged a one-week event for 14 gamblers for Harrah's and was paid $47,500.00 for the job. His prior employment was as a lifeguard at Caesars Palace in Las Vegas in the summer of 1984. He also worked as a ranch hand at Binion's Horse Ranch in Jordan, Montana in the summer of 1981.

Health:
Mr. Chandler reports good health, no major hospitalizations or serious illnesses other than his

alcoholism. He has consumed alcohol and illegal drugs since 1989. He relates that when not in treatment for his alcoholism he drinks daily, about ten drinks. He also goes on binges, drinking in excess of a pint, usually vodka, and some beers. He admits that he gets belligerent, mean, "just plain hateful" and can be cocky, loud, emotional and obnoxious. His drinking started in high school, he associates it with peer pressure and admits that it was fairly minor compared to now.

As for drugs, Mr. Chandler relates heavy use of marijuana in his senior year of high school, up to 10 joints a day, and occasional use now. He admits some use of cocaine, maybe 3 times a year, and a couple of grams a day. He tries to stay away from cocaine because it makes him nauseous.

Of more serious concern is his abuse of Xanax. Mr. Chandler related that he went to a physician with a friend in 1982, listened to his friend describe the symptoms of anxiety to the physician and observed his friend receive a prescription for Xanax. Mr. Chandler has followed this process a number of times over the years, about 16 and has been given prescriptions for Valium and/or Xanax on each occasion. He consumes these drugs while binging on alcohol.

Mr. Chandler relates a long history of residential substance abuse treatment. In fact he has submitted to treatment after every D.U.I. arrest. He related the following treatment history:

Betty Ford Center 1982	2 days
Sioux Falls, SD 1982	15 days

Charter Ridge Hospital- Lexington,
Kentucky 1984   21 days
Hazelton Pioneer House- Plymouth, MN 1987   40 days
Charter Ridge Hospital- Lexington,
Kentucky 1987   29 days
Betty Ford Center- June 1988   21 days
Salvarro Vista Rancho - August 1988   17 days
ASAP- Van Nuys, CA September 1988   11 days

Following his discharge from ASAP program, Mr. Chandler returned to Aspen to enter his plea in this case. He did not follow through on an aftercare program and reported that he experienced another seven or eight day binge between his appearance to enter his plea and his interview with this officer.

Evaluation:
Joseph Daniel Chandler is a 25-year-old Caucasian male before this court for sentencing on his plea of guilty to his first felony conviction. He has pled guilty to criminal impersonation, a Class Five felony, driving under the influence and leaving the scene of an accident. His plea agreement contemplates granting a deferred judgment and sentence in the felony matter.

Mr. Chandler presented himself for our interview about ten minutes late with a partially complete application for probation. He was slightly withdrawn and somewhat apprehensive. During the course of our interview, he relaxed somewhat and apparently decided to provide more information than was initially shared in his application.

This young man, for one reason or another, has never suffered any legal consequences for his illegal behavior. It is apparent that Joseph Chandler has had ample opportunity to address his alcoholism and probably will not look at his addictive behaviors until he is required to look at his ongoing criminal behaviors.

Recommendation:
It is the recommendation of this officer that the court reflect the plea disposition granting the defendant a Deferred Judgment and Sentence on the felony count in this case.
Respectfully submitted on this day of December 1988
Jon Ezequelle
Probation Officer"

He got out of the Aspen jail a month early for good behavior. Mamma and Daddy and I went to get him. He emerged healthy and smiling, looking strong and confident, grabbing each of us for a warm embrace. Chan made a lot of friends in the jail system and they seemed genuinely sad to part with each other. He heartily shook everyone's hand and gave big hugs all around. The officers were just as fond of Chan as his fellow prisoners. We might as well have been picking him up from summer camp. All the counselors and campers were gathering around in a bittersweet moment to help him with bags and supplies and promising to keep in touch. His dorm/jail mates told us how much he helped them and what a difference he made in their lives, getting them to 'work their program' and be positive. They promised each other to meet sometime in Las Vegas.

Twenty-Three

"Even your emotions had an echo in so much space..."

Kentucky March 2003

"I want to know how you have dealt with Chan." With a peculiar coolness, Aunt Toss popped a cracker in her mouth. She had her feet up on the table and one seersuckered leg crossed over the other. Orange tendrils grazed her yellow turtleneck and big round sunglasses covered her eyes.

"Chan was a lot of trouble, Erin," my aunt started in. "And it seemed to me he was very rough on you."

"I don't know," I mumbled under a nervous giggle, "I think it's made me kind of a basket case, but I don't really remember."

The porch next to the Cabin, by the empty pool, now served as my front yard and her back yard. Aunt Toss and Uncle Ben had moved into my grandparent's house when they passed away so now we both found ourselves inhabiting a place that would never truly be ours. Both properties, the house and the Cabin, were riddled with an illustrious history to which the present could never compare. Both properties would forever be overshadowed by the glamour and tragedy that came before.

"I think the problem was," she began, "I remember when Chan was born, I have never seen such frantic, wild adoration as they gave him. It was as if no baby had ever been born the way your Mamma and Daddy carried on. And he was never disciplined that I could see. He stayed up as long as he wanted to. I guess you did, too, when you came along, but you never were the trouble that he was. And I think the divorce was the 'coup d'état'."

The small town still vibrated from my brother's powerful imprint and it seemed now that my relatives were looking to me for an explanation. To hear them say his name with anything but a deep sense of loss got my back up, to hear them say his name with disdain or accusation made me hate them.

"Chan was magnificent but he was so polar. He would be wonderful and precious, and then he could be awful—cruel. The bully stuff was really bad, and he was just a smart ass!"

Aunt Toss turned to Sam, "Did you know Chan?"

"No," he said. "I always wonder if he would have liked me."

"Well, he was gorgeous, big and tall and strong and handsome, he looked like Richard Gere. He had his father's wit and his mother's gentleness. Anybody he was around he usually dominated," she explained. "But something went wrong because he used it in the wrong way."

"What do you think about it?" I asked without expression.

"Just what a shame, what a shame, what a shame, because he had it all but he made everybody very unhappy, Erin. I don't know why you don't know that."

I took a sip of my beer and covered my eyes with my own big, round, glasses.

"It was chaos here!" She went on, as if explaining for the first time, "it was horrible! Pappy almost had a stroke a number of times. Chan just took over his house. He did anything he wanted, blatantly, right in front of him. And you know he shot somebody's house over there on Kentucky Avenue, barely missed the man's head! People were afraid of him, they were afraid he would shoot them!"

"Half the people around here deserve to be shot," I looked away, indignant on behalf of my big brother.

"All this trouble would just come back here," Aunt Toss was now thoroughly heated. "Everybody was gone so it would come back here to Mammy and Pappy. Mammy was just wild! I thought they were both going to have a stroke a number of times. Your Daddy just didn't understand it, I guess. He was out west and wouldn't believe anything that was happening. Ben was literally trying to save lives! Nobody could do anything! We were just helpless."

"It was just awful," she shook her head, winding down. "If it hadn't been for Mammy's and Pappy's ages, I think it would have been different, but it was a real tragedy. The longer it went on, the harder it was to put the brakes on."

"Yeah." I offered.

"I remember when I heard, I called Ben. I was at the Bicycle store and I called him about something and he told me, and I just nearly died. It was like a knife, it was just horrible, horrible." She said.

"Because you knew, in a way, that it was coming?" Sam asked.

"Everybody did." She looked at me. "And I know of course your mother did, and your Daddy too."

As if on cue, the sun burst through a few white puffy clouds escorting Whit and Uncle Ben into the scene. The sky was bluer than any sky I had seen in years and the air was fresh and dewy because of the rain earlier. Taking a seat in the sun, they set down a plate with more crackers and smoked oysters.

"Why do you think Chan wanted to be here in Versailles so bad?" I asked Whit.

"I guess he felt like it was taken away from him," Whit reached a hand up to adjust his John Lennon specs. "The net, the sense of safety, I suppose that was a big issue for him."

Cousins, Ben, Chan, Whit and Matthew Chandler,
Elm Street, Versailles, Kentucky

"He was a divider, not a uniter," Uncle Ben chimed in. "I told him, 'you are about to divide us permanently, your Daddy and me'. And he almost succeeded."

"Well, I'm glad he didn't," I said half-heartedly, eyes closed, face toward the sun.

"Your Daddy wanted to believe everything Chan said. He couldn't believe what I said because I was being critical. But it was what I was seeing with my own eyes!" Uncle Ben continued fervently.

"Louis Mucie showed up with him one day and Chan was beat to a pulp, welts here and there. Chan had started a fight and was so drunk he couldn't defend himself, so he was just swollen and bleeding." This seemed to encourage a tear from Uncle Ben's eyes. I was ready for the sympathy, love and concern for his nephew to pour out. I'm still waiting.

"You know your Daddy told me one time that Chan was the best thing that ever happened to him," Uncle Ben scoffed, dead set on his point of view. "I told your Daddy Chan was the worst thing that ever happened to him. He completely changed when he had to handle Chan and save him from this, that, and the other."

This made my face hot and my chest hurt. Daddy and Chan adored each other like twins might, so much more than father and son. I wanted to play tit for tat, bark about how his three boys grew up in a fishbowl, protected by our grandfather's local celebrity and were still far from perfect. He refused to see the irony and the conversation was going nowhere fast. My face might have been red hot, but my manner remained diminutive.

"It was just important, you know…" I stammered. "To all of us actually… it was just very important for Chan to still be a part of this family even though we were all over. He was just trying to… and since we were all kind of living away and doing other things… it doesn't mean that we weren't still part of the family." I was, at this point, long in the habit of not finishing sentences when nervous, darting out thoughts and images only the proud few could comprehend. Uncle Ben was doing a pretty good job.

"But he was a divider," he repeated.

"Who was a divider?" I asked.

"Chan was a divider. He almost made enemies of the two of us, your Daddy and myself," he said. "And we have had very little trouble since he has been gone. Now that's a sad thing to say."

"I think he just..." my voice trailed off. I was in shock. That was it, my worst fear, my harshest accusation confirmed casually and callously. Hearing my uncle say he was relieved that Chan wasn't around sent chills down my spine. My blood boiled and I went ice cold to him. I was facing an enemy, not part of the tribe. But I had become expert at recognizing these revelations and hiding my distaste and resolution behind a blank stare.

"You all understandably romanticize the situation, because you need to, you want to and you need to," he said gently, pompously, philosophically. "And something catastrophic is going to happen if your Daddy doesn't stop drinking and if he doesn't stop gambling," Uncle Ben whispered. "You'll find yourself visiting the cemetery."

"He's going to live until he's ninety, like Mammy. I want him to leave Las Vegas and come back here and live."

Uncle Ben pointed to a house across the street. "Your Daddy had that house and lost it gambling. And he had your all's place on Elm Street and he lost that too."

"Well he has this now." I looked up at the Cabin that everyone loved but me. "Don't you think that's fair? For Daddy to have something that's his own?"

"Well, sure. I'm ready for Dan to have anything. I even gave him half of my lot over there."

"I'm just glad he has one thing to call his own," I whined. "He's worked so hard, I'm just glad he has something."

"I am too," Uncle Ben laughed. "'Cause he hasn't lost it yet!"

Twenty-Four

*"I never seen you looking so bad my funky one. You tell
me that your super fine mind has come undone..."*

STEELY DAN

Kentucky 1988

I stood in the doorway of the devil room upstairs in the Cabin. It
was 2:00 in the afternoon and Chan sat on the bed in a brown
paisley Ralph Lauren silk robe, his legs crossed Indian style. He
spread out an assortment of colorful pills and popped a few, here
and there.

"Are you trying to kill yourself?" I asked him.

"Yeah." He replied evenly as he looked up, "It's just taking too
long."

The cottage. That's what our childhood friend Julie called it.

"It was when he was living back there in that cottage," she said.
It sounded like a dirty word to me. Chan asked her to marry him.
She was just passing through town and hadn't seen him in years.

"I've had a really rough time of it," he said to her. "For a long
time, years, I've had a really rough time. I'm so tired of living this
way. I don't want to feel this way anymore. Marry me Julie."

He jumped up and got excited. "I promise I will quit all of this if you just say the word right now. Can you imagine what our parents would think if you and I got married?"

"Channy, I can't marry you. I love you but I live in Florida! I don't understand any of this," she looked around the room. "You'll be fine."

"Yeah." He turned his lips up for a smile.

I think he proposed to a lot of girls during that time, grasping for anything and anyone to save him. Each girl thought she was the one. He swaggered around town so handsome and charming, treating every girl like a queen.

"I often think about what it would be like to be married to Chan Chandler," Julie said to me later. "Not so bad."

Twenty-Five

"Desperado, why don't you come to your senses,
you've been out riding fences for so long now…"

EAGLES

Los Angeles 1992
"LA is not my lady!" Chan announced looking out the window at the congested street scene of Lincoln Blvd. We drove together down the merchant packed road that runs through the coastal towns Santa Monica, Venice, Marina, and Playa Del Rey. I had just finished college and started going to acting classes at Playhouse West when I moved into Chan's beautiful one bedroom in Marina Del Rey. There was a sweet little gas fireplace next to the kitchen and sliding glass doors that overlooked the boats in the harbor. My big brother was actually sober and attending Santa Monica College. He was also heavily into his A.A. meetings in the Valley. Since the arrest in Aspen, he was ordered by the courts to stay sober for two years. It had already been a year and a half and all was calm.

Chan gallantly gave up his bedroom for me and slept on the living room floor. He counseled me when I was lonely and gently nudged me away from people he thought might be a bad influence. There were no bar fights, no threatening to throw my cat out the window, no actual throwing of stereos and TV's, just quiet lunches at Hugo's and dinners at Alice's on the pier. Life with no big dramas was a pleasant new experience. It felt slightly disconcerting not to be on the defense from some flying object. This mellow brother who was kind and considerate was somewhat alien to me. It made me shy around him.

Every day we went somewhere fun to eat. We would start off with oysters on the half shell and crab cakes. We laughed and reminisced and indulged in everything fine dining had to offer but I noticed a distinct feeling in the air of, 'I'm here now, but it isn't enough.'

I knew my restless brother was looking down the highway, missing the hot wind in his hair, Corona in his hand and the long road, a blank slate ahead of him. I didn't know exactly what was going on in his head and he certainly didn't know what was swirling around mine but ultimately I felt at home, comforted in his presence. But I could see Chan was unsatisfied, there was a sweet melancholy when he smiled at the waitress and thanked the waiter.

Chan brought me with him to pick up his two-year chip at his regular A.A. meeting in Van Nuys. Walking in, you could see everyone loved him. As usual, he was the most vibrant person in the room. Sauntering through the crowd with his head held high, he proudly introduced me to everyone as his baby sister. I was so proud to be his little sister. I sat on the front row and watched him accept his two-year chip. Chan's short speech was humble, full of charm and wit. He thanked his sponsor Ernesto and went about hugging everyone, accepting congratulations and well wishes. Then he grabbed my hand and led me out the door.

When we arrived home, I went straight to the tiny kitchen and got out the chocolate chip ice-cream cake I got from Baskin-Robbins. It said 'Happy Two Years!' on it. I lit the two candles on top and emerged singing Happy Birthday. We sat on pillows in front of the fireplace and I cut us each a giant piece. Chan took one bite of his and grimaced, investigating what he had just consumed.

"Jesus Fucking Christ!" He shouted before slowly removing one of my cat's hairs from his mouth. He threw the cake down and left the room. The magical evening ended on a sour note. He had stayed sober for two years, for as long as they made him pee in a cup.

Twenty-Six

"Cause if you stay with us you're
gonna' be pretty kooky too..."

DAVID BOWIE

Kentucky April 2003

I started trudging across the street to spend time with Aunt Mimi. I loved being around her. She reminded me of Mammy. I come from a string of extraordinary, strong women on both sides of my family and I knew it was in my blood to pull myself out of this. I just needed a little shove to gather the strength once again, to get on with my life.

We sat on her screened-in porch, drinking whiskey sours out of chilled silver cups, overlooking the field of dandelions and wildflowers that grew in her back yard. Aunt Mimi was a film actress in the forties. She was under contract at Paramount and did a few big movies. In *And the Angels Sing*, she starred with Betty Hutton, Diana Lynn and Dorothy Lamour as one of four singing sisters. I think she was the most beautiful of the four and the best actress and singer, too. She obviously possessed an enormous amount of talent but her career was cut short when against the studio's wishes, she ran off to get married just short of filming her third picture.

"We lived in what we called the little house, are you familiar with the little house?" she asked me.

"No…" I questioned. "I don't think so."

"Well, you need to be." She scrunched up her nose, "you need to be. It was before your father was ever born. That's where the family started."

"It was over there on High Street," she pointed past the field. "This house next door sat over across the street where we lived in between times when Daddy was lieutenant governor. That's where we were until we went to Frankfort. And while we were in Frankfort, when Daddy was governor the second time, they picked the house up and moved it across the street!" She laughed.

"How did you like growing up in the governor's mansion?" I asked.

"Well, now you are talking about something that was bad for me," she ran her hands through her thick silver hair. "It's a really awful thing to find out that your friends only like you because you're the governor's daughter, only because they get to spend the night at the mansion, if you invite them. That was when I was nine to twelve. If young Ben wins, Lucy will be the same age. It's the same four years and she has two younger brothers too!" She was very excited about my cousin's campaign for governor that year. "I am watching the whole thing with great interest, because it happened to us! But I cannot say I spent a happy four years."

"Really?" I listened.

"Mother and Daddy were so busy, they hardly had any time to talk to us at all, particularly Daddy. You know, Daddy wondered, when he got really old, why Mother was everyone's favorite. Well, we hardly knew him! And he didn't understand that. He was always saying, 'Why don't they like me like they like her?' Well!" She vivaciously announced, "it's because she spent every waking minute with us and he didn't!"

I loved hearing stories of Mammy and Pappy before we all came along. It was hard to picture my stout grandmother who seemed to have been born in her seventies with a head full of auburn curls, young and glamorous, hosting parties at the Governor's mansion. I only saw her later in life, when she dressed in various housecoats puttering around the garden and sat at her mahogany desk writing her weekly column for *The Woodford Sun*.

"The first four years as first lady Mother was busy doing her own thing. She had three bridge clubs," she held up her fingers, "Three! Mother had a wonderful time. Mother and Daddy were busy, always very busy. They went to receptions, they went to balls, they went to this, that and the other. They went out of town and we just had people who looked after us. So it was just not a happy time for me. As a matter of fact, it was sort of a sad time."

First Lady, Mildred Watkins Chandler with children, Dan (in her lap), Ben, Mimi and Marcella, Governors Mansion, Frankfort, Kentucky

Aunt Mimi only let her melancholy linger for moments before her strong, defensive side returned, "I think Dan and Ben had a wonderful time. Everything revolved around them. They had all these kids that came and played football and baseball in the afternoons. You see, I didn't have any of that. I'm not going to say I was miserable. I don't remember being miserable. But I don't remember being terribly happy either. I always wanted more attention from my parents than I got... always," said the actress.

I went into the kitchen to fill my silver cup with a few more thimbles of bourbon. I passed her photos on the wall, her publicity shots from Paramount Pictures, Mammy as a beautiful young girl in the 20s, Daddy, an adorable three year old on Pappy's shoulders in front of a cheering crowd at a political rally.

"Bring in those nuts, will you, honey?" she called.

"I can remember one of the things that made me unhappy to my core was that I would be at the dinner table." In an impromptu interpretive dance she moved her hands in the air, "I'd be holding court and talking about this happened and that happened, and all of a sudden Daddy would say, 'Put something in your mouth and chew it.'"

I realized at that moment we had grown up with the same father.

"It's like my dad! Daddy does that to me!" I screeched.

"Well, your Daddy got it, all right. That male chauvinism thing, he got. He came by it honestly. Neither of them care a ding-dong about women as a general classification. Daddy was a man's man and a boy's boy and didn't pay a whole lot of attention to Marcella or me. We were Mother's to handle!"

Daddy and Pappy could both be totally insensitive and neither believed something coming out of a woman's mouth could be of any great importance.

"I would run from the table in tears! I can hear Mother now saying, 'Happy, aren't you ashamed of yourself to hurt her feelings like that, just trying to tell a story!'" Aunt Mimi pulled her little dog Lilly, up to her lap.

"Everything with me was a big drama, big drama, and Mother and Daddy both thought I wanted to be an actress, but I didn't. I really never did, and you see, they were both frustrated actors, both of them."

"That's not how it was!" my father later balked. "Daddy was a U.S. Senator at the time! He wasn't gonna' leave the Senate for the movies!" he snorted. "You talk to Mimi and you won't think you're talking about the same family."

"Daddy loved working for the movie people!" Aunt Mimi went on. "You see, there was not a movie section of the state government and they had to ask Daddy if he would arrange it so they could take scenes at Churchill Downs, and so on and so forth. He arranged it all."

The acting career fell onto Aunt Mimi's lap when the director, David Butler became close friends with Pappy when he came to town to film the movie *Kentucky*. Every time they had company, Mammy would crank up the record player, place Mimi in the middle of the room and have her perform. When David Butler came to the mansion for dinner, they cranked up the record player, paraded Mimi out to the middle of the room and had her sing two songs. Mr. Butler was so impressed he told Mammy if she ever got to Hollywood, he would do a screen test.

"Mother and Daddy thought I had the best voice of anybody in the whole world. Mother would have been wonderful in light opera. I don't think her voice was heavy enough for Grande Opera," she speculated. "But Light Opera, she would have been just wonderful. But, you know she chose another path in life. Daddy thought he was the best singer in the whole world too, always did... and he wasn't."

In 1942, Mammy and Aunt Mimi took a train to California for my Aunt Marcella's wedding to a pilot named Jack Greg. "Gloria Vanderbilt was her maid of honor. I bet you didn't know that!" Aunt Mimi said. "She was marrying Pat DiCicco and he was a good friend of Jack's. Anyway, they had a tiny little wedding. It was beautiful. And since we were in Hollywood for the wedding, Mother looked up David Butler and we all went to dinner. That night he said we should do that screen test." My grandmother was ecstatic.

"OOOOOHHHH! That would be great!" Mammy said.

Matt Dennis, who wrote *Angel Eyes* and *Can't Get Started With You*, helped Mimi pick out three songs to sing. They were back in Kentucky when three weeks later David Butler called to say Paramount wanted to put Mimi under contract. Mammy was thrilled. Aunt Mimi was bummed, "I was going to be a cheerleader!" She laughed, "I was going to make it!"

This was in October and she was before the cameras in December making *Henry Aldridge Swings It*.

Mimi Chandler, Hollywood publicity shot

A six-page spread in *Life* magazine featuring Pappy and Aunt Mimi read:

'A.B. 'Happy' Chandler for the next seven years as United States Senator from Kentucky, and his daughter Mimi Chandler for the next seven years under contract at Paramount.'

"Mammy was a writer in Hollywood, right?" I asked her.

"Mother didn't write diddly squat!" Aunt Mimi grumbled. "Mother made the most out of the littlest thing you could possibly imagine. Harry Brand was a good friend of David Butler's so they were introduced. She let him know that she was out here but her husband was back in Washington D.C. as a Senator. Well, they need senators," she leaned in conspiratorially, "they *need* senators. So really, as a lark more than anything else, he asked her to read books and let him know if she thought one of them would make a good movie. Well, she did that for about six months. But to hear her tell it, you would think she did it for six years! Big deal!" It's this attitude that earned Aunt Mimi the nickname, 'Mustard' among my cousins.

"Anyway, I didn't stay very long because Jack and Marcella were living in Palm Springs and I went down to visit them and met Johnny Cable," she said of her first husband. She was just 17.

"He asked me to marry him in March, we got married in June and I never went back to the movies!" She threw up her hands.

"That's another thing Ben and Dan got mad about," she pouted. "Your Uncle Ben said to me once, 'Mother and Daddy went to so much expense to bring you out there and get you an apartment, and in two years you were gone. You didn't even live up to your contract!'" She was stung by my uncle's comments. "Well, I feel really bad about that now," she apologized to me. "I really do."

"What did they say at the studio?" I asked of her packing up and leaving.

"I had already done the costume fittings for my third movie when I got married, a movie called *Out of This World*, and I never even went to the first day! I ran into this big legal thing upstairs the other day when I was looking through some old papers. I found this document from O'Melveny and Meyers, the legal firm, saying, 'You cannot make movies for anybody. Period!' because I had walked out on my contract."

"So you did just walk out." I said.

"I just walked out, I did nothing!" she shrugged.

We contemplated that for a moment, listening to the birds chirp and the frogs talk from the creek nearby.

"Who did you have to tell?" I pressed delicately, still trying to get the full picture.

"Nobody…" she winced. "I just left! But when they found out I wasn't coming back for the movie I had started…" she shook her head.

"You know, I think I thought I was going back," she whispered. "I really do think I thought I was going back, but Johnny wanted me to stay with my parents while he was overseas ferrying planes over the hump in India. So I just left. I don't remember how my mind worked back then but not very well, I know that!"

Happy Chandler with daughter Mimi and first husband
Johnny Cable, Stork Club, New York City

She was philosophical, as if realizing for the very first time, "I didn't think about things like that, I just did whatever I wanted to do. And Mother and Daddy made the mistake of always allowing me to do whatever I wanted to do. That's a big mistake," she stared at me. "You need to discipline children, you need to teach them right from wrong. They didn't do any of that, either of them. They just assumed that everybody knew everything, but apparently I didn't know a whole lot about anything!"

"Are you happy here?" I asked. "Do you ever miss the movie business?"

"Honey, I wouldn't do what you're doing if they *gave* me Hollywood!" she said.

"But do you ever wish you lived someplace a little more exotic?" I couldn't believe she would be satisfied in Versailles. I assume it was just good old-fashioned security that kept her here all these years, the same thing Chan wanted.

"All I ever wanted was to be a good mother and a good wife, neither of which worked out! My kids are *not* what I ordered from the pet store. The great ambition of my life was to be considered by my husband the best wife in the world and considered by my children the best mother in the world and I didn't get either one. My children do not think I'm the best mother and I was married to my husband for twenty years and he never thought I was the best wife."

Then she held her head up and smiled, "I thought to myself not too long ago, you know, piss on it! It just didn't happen for me the way I wanted it to."

Twenty-Seven

*"I'm just living on nerves and feelings, with a
weak and a lazy mind and coming to people's
parties fumbling deaf dumb and blind..."*

JONI MITCHELL

Kentucky May 2003

"Ben, Ben! Ben! BeeeeeeeeYoooooooooooooNnnnnnnnn!!
Benny, Benny! Beeeeeyooooon! Ben!" Daddy rocked back
and forth in a rocking chair on the porch of the Cabin, yelling for
his brother next door.

"Tossy! Tossy! Tooooossssssyyyyyy, Toss! Toss! Toss!" He tried
for Aunt Toss.

He spotted his sister at the end of the lawn walking her dog,
"Mimi! Get over here Mimi! Mimi! Mimi!! Look at her. She's not
gonna come."

I adored my father but he truly drove me batty. The sense of
responsibility I felt was overwhelming. The pressure to make sure
he wasn't lonely, that he was happy and healthy, and the guilt of not
doing a bang up job left me exhausted. Daddy forever demanded
excitement. We had to be talking about the next big thing. There
was always some guy he had just met who was going to put me in

this movie or that TV show, or he was about to make millions on a random deal, or he was flying to the Bahamas, or planning an enormous party. We always had to be on the verge of something extraordinary.

It was vitally important for him to ingrain in us this notion of having as much fun as possible at all times. Consequently, Chan drove from one end of the country to the other and I spent years bursting into tears if my friends wanted to go home early. We never wanted the party to end. Valentine's Day had to be perfect. My birthday? Forget about it. "I don't know whose birthday this is, but it sure isn't mine," I whimpered after another less than astonishing evening.

Daddy tried to make everything fabulous— at the last minute. Christmas was usually Chan, Daddy, me, one of his secretaries and some other odd stranger. We'd sit on the carpet of some painfully unfurnished house and Daddy would enthusiastically break out the Dom Perignon, then run around playing Santa Claus, passing out a slew of unwrapped presents he bought that morning.

Now it was my turn to make everything perfect, to gloss over the chaos, to Razzle Dazzle 'em. Daddy and I were in a state of disrepair. We were like two lost pieces of a puzzle and the puzzle wasn't even good anymore because some of the pieces were missing so the picture was doomed from the start.

One disapproving look of his could make me feel like such an asshole and make every insecurity come pouring back. I wanted to be the kind of daughter he wanted me to be but I also needed to become the kind of person that felt organic to my soul. I could never find a comfortable balance.

In a pathetic attempt to fix everything, I decided to paint the pool and fill it with water before Daddy's annual fried chicken party, the day after the Kentucky Derby. I wanted everything to be perfect for his friends flying in from California, Arkansas and Vegas. I wanted them to see a stylish and elegant Dan Chandler and the lovely family that surrounded him.

It was just a week away when I got the idea so I had to work fast. I called Swoop Daddy, the liquor storeowner down the street and asked him to come over. I told him the pool hadn't been painted in 30 years and I was desperate to paint it immediately.

He took one look at the empty pool filled with leaves and moss and said, "You need to get some Mexicans over here."

"Oh, okay," I said.

"Yeah, I know some guys who can come over, maybe later on today, and clean this out. Does that drain work?"

"I think so." I searched the deep end looking for the drain.

"Okay," Swoop continued. "Well, I brought this book of colors, look through this and pick out a color. Once they've cleaned it, I'll get these guys to paint it."

"I just want it blue, light blue... like a nice blue. We probably need to start on it today, don't you think?" I pushed. "So it will be done this weekend? Can we do that?"

"Well, we're gonna' see aren't we?" He flirted. "I've gotta make some calls."

Daddy came out by the pool with his cigar and Scotch and looked suspiciously at Swoop.

"So what's goin' on here? What's the plan? Hey uh... Swoop... I don't want any of those original tiles touched. They've been there since 1949 and I don't want any shit tiles replacin' em."

"Daddy, it's fine," I panicked. "He's gonna get some guys to clean out the pool and paint it but we have to let him do what he knows how to do."

"I just don't want any of those original tiles touched, those are good tiles, I don't want any shit tiles put in their place," he repeated.

"Well, those are pretty old," Swoop attempted to school my father. "You're gonna need to get somebody to come and scrape along those so all that comes off along the side."

"Hey, buddy," Daddy snapped. "Don't tell me what I need! I need a lot of things. I need trees along those fences. I need a lot of things!"

Sweat dripped off Swoop's ruddy face and soaked his t-shirt as he defended himself, "well, maybe you're not ready for me to get a crew over here if you don't know what you want."

"Hey, buddy, I know what I want." My dad barked. "Don't do me any favors. Erin Lynne, I'm gonna' get one of Talbot's boys over here. You can tell this man we don't need anything from him."

"Daddy!" I pleaded as he walked back into the Cabin.

Swoop looked down, looked around, took a sip of his beer and gathered himself.

"You know, honey, your dad is treating me like a piece of shit, and I'm notta' piece a shit. I'm not gonna' have anybody treatin' me like that in front of my guys."

"He's just really obnoxious sometimes," I apologized. "Don't take it personally."

"I'm notta' piece a shit," he said again before storming off across the yard. I'm not gonna' have anybody treatin' me like I'm some piece a shit!"

"He looked a little goofy," Daddy said when I got back in the Cabin. "He had that red eyed look. That red eyed, glassy look."

"Daddy, he owns a liquor store in Versailles, what do you expect?"

Later that night my father called Swoop and said he was sorry for offending him, but the damage was done. We had three days left to paint and fill the pool before everyone arrived. I was the only one who saw the urgency in this. Sam and Daddy didn't care at all but I was frantic for the place to look put together. I was also personally tired of looking at a big, ugly, empty, rotting hole in the ground. I needed to brighten up the atmosphere. I wanted to swim and dangle my feet in clear, peaceful, soothing water.

I pushed and pushed and pushed until finally Sam and I were in the pool, fighting, sweating, swearing and painting. We painted feverishly in the sticky humidity until we were covered in blue paint and all nine cans were gone. It was ridiculously typical that we would run out of paint before the pool was finished. Now, it looked more white trash than when we started. The sides were bright blue while the floor was left a dirty, white unpainted mess. Of course, the old 1949 tiles were still intact in all their mildewy glory.

Meanwhile, in the shallow end, I shared a bottle of white wine with my dad who periodically looked down and laughed, "That looks great!" He said, actually meaning it. "Erin Lynne, my baby!"

There were only a few strokes of paint left when, in an act of true passive aggression, Sam demonically wrote Derby 2003 in huge letters on the bottom of the pool. He said he thought it looked cool, but I knew he did it to spite me. He was sure this would add just enough tackiness to send me over the edge. As usual, we looked like the Beverly Hillbillies. How we managed to be the biggest hillbillies in Versailles was a mystery, but we did a good job.

It was about this time that I started having uncontrollable fits of absolutely jumping out of my skin. I began a private little ritual of throwing something against the wall with all my force and then listening quietly, hoping Daddy and Sam didn't hear me. I didn't want to see the indignant 'what the hell is wrong with you' look on their faces.

I felt like Blanche Dubois, stuck in the Cabin. I wanted to crouch down with the phone and whisper, "danger, danger!!" I also developed some newfound lockjaw. I kept tensing up my chin until all the tension in my body was focused in my chin. My LA neurosis had nothing on this. I was quite literally a basket case.

The next day the guests arrived. Not surprisingly, I was burnt out and hung over. John Smith was the first of the out-of towners to land. The Las Vegas reporter wrote a book about my dad, called *Bluegrass Days, Neon Nights*. John had followed Daddy around for years, soaking up decades of his hard won insider information about the gaming industry. Daddy was both a witness to and a historian of Vegas from its inception to the Disneyland it is today. My father was sparing when it came to divulging details of his personal life in the book but he recounted many fascinating stories of the connected casino bosses that used to run the town. He shared hilarious tales of his high times with world-renowned sports legends and music icons as well as the private world of the most notorious high rollers. Of course, like in everything Daddy did, there was a healthy dose of Pappy and all things Kentucky.

I wanted to make a good impression on this writer. I failed to take into account that in following my dad around for so long he had probably already formed a pretty solid opinion. I was anxious for John Smith to see his subject as happy and successful and surrounded by loved ones. Instead, when he arrived we were already drunk and I was too exhausted to be a hostess. I threw out a bag of chips and salsa and a few peanuts and let him fend for himself. Then I filled my glass with wine and sat outside in a rocking chair with a smile plastered on my face.

Instead of the exquisite home life I dreamed of portraying, Daddy and I ended the evening with a knockdown drag-out fight in front of everyone because I wanted to go out and he didn't want me to. My music was blaring when he stumbled into my room, red faced and hostile, drunkenly yelling. I sobbed to my friend Connie, who was in town from LA for the 'festivities.' I told her how miserable I was and how I would go insane if I stayed much longer. We put on quite an opening night show.

The next morning, I rushed out to the grocery to get every type of sweet roll and muffin in stock. I made eggs and bacon and sausage biscuits and put out a huge spread. As the guests came down, I greeted them with a smile, lowered eyes and an unhealthy amount of guilt and humiliation bubbling below the surface.

The rest of the weekend was loud and raucous as a conglomeration of lawyers, coaches, bookies and ex-NFL stars drank from the moment they woke up until the moment they fell into bed. There was lots of Neanderthal male bonding, with insults and compliments flying simultaneously over cigars and Scotch. Daddy held court and was the loudest of them all. His favorite target was his best friend and lawyer.

"There is one among us who wants to be the bride at every wedding and the corpse at every funeral! Dick Crane, please shut up!"

Saturday morning, Buzzy Nave's tricked out bus came to take them all to Louisville for the Derby. Sam and I were invited but chose to stay home. It was the first time in a month we were left alone so we decided to take the time to be quiet. We had a wonderful, romantic day and took full advantage of the peace we so desperately needed. But by eight-o-clock that night, the door burst open.

"Dick Crane is a serial liar!" and they were off.

The morning of the party, I woke early to greet Myrtle, the fabulous cook who had come to prepare the feast. She made fried chicken, mashed potatoes, green beans and corn pudding for 150 people. I placed sterling silver goblets on the tables, lit candles and put Bobby Darin on the stereo. Then I went straight for the red wine. People started filing in about eleven in the morning for our afternoon chicken party. I stayed close to the kitchen and ate livers as soon as Myrtle fried them up.

The guests ate a lot and drank a lot. Daddy made toasts around the pool and everyone laughed, then he introduced my cousin Ben who made a political speech. I sipped red wine poolside—or rather pond side, with the same smile mortared on my face. We had been pumping water into the pool for two days and it was still only half full so I sprinkled flower petals in it, to make it look like it was supposed to be that high. It was pretty cool, but more like a pond. My friend Judi came up and handed me some sort of horse tranquilizer and I casually popped it in my mouth.

The pill hit me like a ton of bricks, put me right out at three in the afternoon. Before I totally crashed, I made my way to the bedroom like Sharon Stone in *Casino*. I locked the door behind me and got into bed, missing the second half of the party.

If I could have done it over—if I could have been the me I knew was buried beneath all the other crap—it would have been lovely. I would not have stressed about the pool. I would not have felt responsible for my father's reputation or for what his friends thought of him. I would have simply straightened up and placed a few decorations around, quietly supporting my husband and father. I would have taken a bubble bath with lavender and eucalyptus then slid into the social arena with the ease and confidence of a princess opening her home... before summering in Portofino.

I spent the next day on the couch, confused, embarrassed and burnt out from the whole week. Thankfully Daddy and his friends flew to the Bahamas to sail on a yacht for a few days. Whit and Mathew came over and I made them recount everything they saw me do, hoping I hadn't done anything too mortifying. They didn't notice a thing, thought it was a good party, blah blah blah. Still, I lay tortured, upside down on the couch. My head was a prison and I gave myself Chinese water torture.

John Smith wrote about it in the *Las Vegas Review Journal*:

> **"On that first Saturday in May, Dan's man Bob Baffert took War Emblem to victory in the Derby. It was a win that placed the Hall of Fame trainer on the top of the thoroughbred racing world. Baffert eschewed the international limelight the next day and drove out to Versailles to Dan's near-famous after-Derby fried chicken picnic. Celebrities from the horseracing world mixed with politicians and plain folks. They filled his big cabin, poured out across the lawn, and lived a little bit larger because of their man, Dan.**
>
> **The whiskey was prime, the chicken sublime, but they really came to hear Dan work the crowd like a cross between a revival preacher and Don Rickles. He can build up a man's character and playfully assassinate it as fast as any nightclub comic.**
>
> **Everyone I met that day hung on each word of Dan's homespun soliloquies, which usually began with 'It's like my Daddy said...' His Daddy invariably said something that rang true as a bell and was side-splittingly funny."**

Sounds fun, wish I had been there. I obviously didn't ruin it, anyway. What made me think I had such an influence on the event in the first place? It didn't matter what I painted, or put on display. My guilt attack lasted until about ten o'-clock that night. Finally, my normal head started to creep back alive and I realized I wasn't such a horrible person. I understood why people want to throw themselves off buildings at times like these. If they only knew if they just hung on a few more hours, things change. Suddenly, your mind shifts and you think, it's really not such a big deal after all is it? *"Any major dude will tell you..."*

Twenty-Eight

"Baby don't want me around..."

MICHAEL PENN

Kentucky May 2003 – Depression Sinks In
"If you are going to start crying again..." Sam said, looking at my sad face.

Approaching the echoing Cabin living room, I saw my young husband's eyes were distant and cold. I stood in the kitchen doorway and tried to think of something positive to say but my mind failed me. Before I knew it, tears welled up just as he predicted. I casually turned and started back into the other part of the house. I was embarrassed and frustrated and above all I had no control over the flood of tears that seemed to have no end.

My communication with Sam was gone. We were no longer in this together. I resented my father for the fact that my marriage was beginning to suck. I resented the fact that the only unconditional love came from my Daddy, not my husband. I was still that little girl up on Gila Monster Mountain outside of Las Vegas. Sam was just some guy that stood outside our impenetrable family unit. Husband was just a word, even saying it made me feel like a fraud. *There are very few people in this life that you can count on. There are very few people in this life you can trust.* I felt this in my gut but I was hanging on to the role of wife with everything I had, which was not much.

My lack of emotional skills drove me further and further into the bottle. I was paralyzed with a rising fear that this relationship was slipping through my fingers. The one thing I had outside the madness of my family, the one thing escorting me away from the herd was turning on me.

"I'm getting awfully tired of watching you get drunk every day, I'll tell you that." Sam said as I walked out of the living room.

This cut me like a knife. I got back into bed, surrounded by tissues and cigarettes and an old glass of red wine. I imagined seeping a razor deep into my veins like in the movie, pushing it all the way in and letting my blood gush out. I was coming apart amidst a haze of Scotch and cigars, wisecracks and insults from my overbearing father, crawling out of my skin in this big dark Cabin with all these memories. My spirit was demolished in this tiny town surrounded by its tiny ideas, and my family with their sweet, put-a-ton-of bricks-in-your-pocket-and-keep-you-down ways.

I went upstairs and looked through the drawers and closets of each of the six bedrooms. Sifting through old pictures, I found one of Chan and me in Lubbock, holding each other tight, Del Estrada, the brown duplex where we lived was in the background. It was a slightly depressing photo of us in high school in the dusty plains of West Texas, grasping the only thing we knew to be true, each other. Our eyes were still hopeful but undoubtedly fragile.

I sat in the devil room in Chan's old closet for hours. The closet he claimed anyway. On the top shelf in the back was a brown leather briefcase. I pulled it down, ready to be showered with pot seeds and loose bullets but what I found were carefully cut out newspaper clippings of his mistakes, "Man Faces Sentencing for Seventh DUI in Aspen," "Casino Executive's Son Detained and Charged with Disturbing the Peace."

It was filled with these letters from the Aspen arrest and other reports of substance abuse. There were copies of complaints from casinos, charges of disturbing the peace and other detailed descriptions of insanity. There were countless letters from lawyers pleading with him, countless letters from lawyers congratulating him on his progress and potential.

The letters addressed from me had their own special place in the brief case. I opened up the handwritten pages and saw my own familiar scrawl, begging him to take care of himself. "I need you," I said over and over. "I need my brother here on earth with me," I pleaded in another. There was a photo album with pictures of us smiling when we were young, clinging to each other out of sheer happiness, no hint of sadness like the later ones.

I found letters from Sister Mary Immaculate, his second grade teacher from St. Leo who loved him dearly, as well as Alcoholics Anonymous meeting directories and Narcotics Anonymous meeting directories from Los Angeles, Las Vegas, Kentucky, and Arizona. Letters from my mom, letters from me, letters from the guys in jail saying they will meet him in Mexico to continue the party and thanking him for the food, clothes and money.

When I closed Chan's briefcase I was exhausted. I began to get drunk every day. I couldn't handle the feeling of stuck-ness I was having. Sam wasn't playing music. His heavy routine of home improvement shows was taking all his time and attention. I wandered around wondering who on earth I was, and how in the world we got there. I was claustrophobic and couldn't stand to be inside. The Cabin was a black hole and there wasn't an inch where I felt comfortable. My only peace came sitting outside on the porch looking through the trees, having a glass of wine and a cigarette. I tried moving the furniture around and redecorating our room. I lit candles and incense. I listened to music. I cooked. I sat on the kitchen counter for hours on end but nothing worked.

I was deeply unhappy and I thought to myself, 'this must be what manic depression is. I'm so sad I can't breathe. I'm depressed and fat and I have a cold. I'm sick and tired and I think I'm dying.' Then the next day it would flip, 'I'm sooooooooo happy! I can't believe how happy I am!' I ran around the Cabin in a frenzy think-ing, 'I'm not looking for anything! I'm not waiting for some time in the future! I'm ecstatic now! How on earth did this happen? I am totally and completely comfortable with myself and my envi-ronment right here and now. I don't want to be anywhere else! I'm so strangely happy! I think I understand. I have the Power of Now!!!' I jumped from room to room, looking at pictures on the wall and grinning from ear to ear.

Then I fell again, curled up in bed, weeping. I hid my distorted face under the covers and wailed. I had no idea why. Sam was exas-perated. He wasn't sure how to get us out of this mess either. His good ole Irish method was to stuff everything down and shut off. He sank deeper and deeper into his own depression and deeper and deeper into the big screen TV. His new station was the red leather chair upstairs in the devil room, a fog of bad energy hover-ing over him. There my husband sat, in my least favorite room in the universe, watching *Trading Spaces* and *While You Were Out*.

With his withdrawing, I became more and more alone and a form of self-destruction I had yet to experience tapped me on the shoulder. Suddenly I had the urge to cut myself and I began to fantasize about beating my head against the wall. The only thing I actually did was slam my blow dryer into the bathroom door, put-ting a deep hole into the flimsy drywall.

A package arrived from Victoria's Secret, as I was still holding on to a tiny semblance of wanting to be pretty and sexy for my husband. The dress I had ordered didn't fit because I had gained so much weight. I ripped it off my body and tore it to shreds with my bare hands. I started doing this regularly with clothes, whenever something didn't look good, I would either calmly tear it in half or rip it to pieces with force. This gave me a few seconds of pleasure. Then I felt like a big idiot. Without enough passion to care, I tossed the shreds in the corner in slow motion and sank back under the covers.

I was so sorry. I felt like such an awful person, an awful wife, an awful companion, a loser who didn't get it, who kept making the same mistakes over and over again, that is the definition of insanity. I kept thinking alcoholism is boring. Depression is boring. People that have it should fix it. There are places you can go to fix such personality defects and everyone can sit in a circle and laugh about how fucked up it all got. I should never drink. I'm confused enough in the head already to voluntarily add this to my list of whatever. I'm really just a periodically crazy person, but when it pops up, it really pops up and this new despair was worse than ever, the grief and guilt was overwhelming.

Twenty-Nine

"From Sea to Shining Sea..."

*K*ATHARINE *L*EE *B*ATES

Kentucky May 2003 - Democratic Primary

Somehow Sam and I found ourselves standing on a stage in front of a giant American flag with balloons dropping on our heads. In fact, my entire family stood in front of that flag before thousands of cheering people. It was the Democratic Primary convention in Louisville.

It was Ben's big day, and we all joined in support to find out if my cousin had gotten the democratic nomination for governor. Everyone met at the Cabin to wait for Buzzy and Linda Nave who were taking us up in his fancy bus. Uncle Ben and Aunt Toss held hands as they walked over from next door, every bit the nervous and proud parents of the man of the hour. Whit and Mathew were actually on time and looking snazzy in their suits and ties. Aunt Mimi clipped across the street all dressed up, looking tres chic. Daddy was already sweating profusely as he wrangled the crowd. We climbed on the bus and set out for Louisville to count the votes. I was pretty drained from getting ready and I was starving to boot so when our host broke out sandwiches and start mixing drinks, I perked up. I couldn't decide whether to have wine, beer or a Bloody Mary.

"Rein it in there, Jane," Sam said.

I hadn't even begun. I knew I had to be cool, tonight especially, but I was uncomfortable and didn't really want to go, besides. I felt fat in my white skirt and flowy green top. I wanted to be in jeans and a T-shirt in LA, having a margarita at El Coyote. Instead, I dutifully smiled and tried to be a good little cousin of the next would-be governor.

Everyone was nervous. Daddy had been tirelessly raising money for Ben's campaign. This was something he understood very well, politics and rallies and public speaking. He should have done it himself. My father was tailor made for this life. He could talk in front of a crowd all day, keeping an audience transfixed with his sharp insights and hilarious banter. "My Daddy used to say…" then he would say something he used to say, giving away the credit. He never tired of giving his audience an enormous kick.

We got to the hotel and ran into our friend Judi, who promptly led Sam and me to the bar, holding our hands and guiding us through the politically charged crowd. I got a glass of wine, and before long we were ushered upstairs to a suite where we waited out the last hour of the vote counting. The tension was unbelievable. Daddy, Ben and Uncle Ben sat transfixed to the TV. Several young preppy handlers in khaki pants and blue paisley ties ran around with a desperate sense of importance and urgency. They whispered into their cell phones and gripped their clipboards. Sam, Whit and Mathew stood out on the balcony, chatting casually a million stories up. I sat on the couch staring at them, praying they would come in. There was only that familiar, flimsy little iron rail to keep them from falling to their death. It made my knees weak and my stomach sink.

Ben had run an impressive campaign but the race was close. Over the last few months, he stayed cool and collected, winning every debate. He was tough as nails and stuck to his guns. Now was the moment of truth. He looked like a textbook politician with his beautiful wife, Jennifer, and three of the cutest kids you have ever seen.

"They look like they came from central casting." Judi said. "You couldn't have dreamed up a more perfect looking governor's family." She was right. They looked the cookie-cutter image of what America would want. It was an ideal picture. He had worked his whole life for this. Ben had been Kentucky's attorney general for years with a law enforcing, money saving, family-oriented reputation. Never doing anything that might stand in the way of his goals, he cared about the land and the people of his state. He seemed destined for this since he was born and given the name Albert Benjamin Chandler III.

I wanted him to win for Aunt Toss more than anything else. Kentucky could use a woman like her in the Governor's mansion. To have an artist in the public eye who was interesting and funny. Mad crazy for people in general, she campaigned for her son going to each little town wearing funny hats and pins. Her tireless energy knew no bounds as she ran from one event to the next. Aunt Toss could effortlessly find something fascinating about each new face in the hollers of the Kentucky Mountains. A passionate activist for decades, she was rabid on the subject of keeping the land as nature intended, violently opposing any building or development in Woodford County. Along with former first lady, Libby Jones, Aunt Toss was successful in protecting the picturesque land we call home.

Kentucky had been Ben's home for generations before and will be for generations after. Who better than he to take a stand and make Kentucky the best it can be? Who better than he to look after it? Who cared more? This was his life and his home. It's my home too. This is who I am and this is my family. I felt all these things and more. I was proud, excited and an integral part of it all. I had another glass of wine and Sam reprimanded me, "You are just determined to fuck up, aren't you?"

No. I wasn't. I only wanted a glass of wine. I was being as calm and cool as I possibly could. I felt I was playing the part of support-ive family member pitch perfect. I was certainly praying for Ben to win. I was also very proud of myself for not bringing the pot I had in my drawer back in the Cabin. I was eyeing the hallways in the hotel and was sure I would have thought I could get away with sneak-ing off into a corner and taking a few hits. Pot surely would have made more bearable the frozen, demure smile I had plastered on my face for the last three hours. That would have been bad, me getting arrested. That would have made everyone really, really mad. So, as I sipped my red wine quietly, I thought I was doing a good job.

Someone burst into the suite and announced that Ben had won. Everyone hugged and cheered. I grabbed Aunt Toss and we jumped up and down screaming. Ben hugged me and told me he loved me. I told him I loved him too. The two of us have had a distant, slightly uncomfortable relationship in the past. He is a few years older than Chan and they were extremely close, best friends and rivals, depending on the day. They were the good boy and the bad boy. Chan idolized Ben and respected him for his stead-fast ways and ability to do the right thing. I resented him for that because I assumed the admiration wasn't reciprocated. Years ago when they were in college, Ben came over to Chan's apartment one morning. Chan was rolling a joint.

"Roll one down with me, Hanny." Chan offered.

Ben scoffed and shook his head haughtily. "Now why would I want to do that? Why would I do that and ruin my whole day?"

I remember thinking, if his day is going to be ruined, why shouldn't yours be? Fiercely loyal to my tribe.

Ben made an acceptance speech and I clapped along with everyone else. Aunt Toss and Uncle Ben stood strong and united. Daddy squeezed my hand and laughed with big tears in his eyes. Our funny little dysfunctional family created a wonderful scene. Carrying the torch seemed fitting and natural and perfect. I wish Mammy and Pappy were there to see it, and I know they were.

Thirty

*"When the sun came up it was another day, when
the sun went down you were blown away..."*

LUCINDA WILLIAMS

Kentucky May 1993

We waited in the lobby of Milward's Funeral Home. The service was for our grandfather. My mom's father, Daddy Gene lay a few feet away and Mamma wouldn't go in.

"Where's my son?" She cried. "Where's Channy? Where's my son?"

Chan rushed in out of the rain, looking handsome as ever in a gray designer suit. With his head held high and a soft smile on his face, he came prepared to take care of his mom. Enveloping her in his lanky embrace, she melted into his arms and he ushered her into the viewing room. I followed them in slowly as we said our last good-byes to our dear grandfather.

Chan and I were behind the funeral home smoking a cigarette when a girl in a pretty pink dress and pearls walked up. I think we knew her when we were kids. She opened up her hand and showed Chan a joint. He hugged me and was off.

The next day we went to Daddy Gene's house in Lexington with the whole family from my mom's side. Chan showed up late in his long black leather coat and poked his head in the door. He looked almost too big for the house, too big for the world. He gathered up our cousins Katie, Brandon, Brad and me for dinner.

We sat somberly at our table at TGI Fridays. I was sad, but deeply comforted to be at the table with my big brother who sat at the end talking to Brad with his legs crossed and a long, black coat wrapped around him. I looked at my beautiful cousins who could be the on the cover of a fashion magazine, a Calvin Klein advertisement all three, tan and chiseled. It's funny that we're family, I thought, Chan and I are so different. We aren't perfect looking like they are… but we sure are cool. I'm glad we're us. I smiled at Chan and thought, *I love us.*

When we got up to leave, Chan hugged me and kissed my cheek. I told him I had something for him and placed a little silver guardian angel pin in his palm. He smiled, kissed it and closed his hand tightly around the charm, "Erin Lynne, I'm gonna be your guardian angel."

Two weeks later Los Angeles – May 18th 1993

I was on the floor of my apartment on Sycamore doing yoga when Chan called.

"Hey, Kid," he said

"Hey! What are you doing?" I jumped up, excited to hear from him.

"I'm watching *The Money Pit.* It's funny as shit!" He laughed and I laughed along with him.

"You know when he's stuck in the floor, and the guy comes over, and he's yelling for him to help and the guy goes, 'I can hear you in there laughin' at me!" We both laughed hysterically and repeated, "I can hear you in there laughin' at me!"

I asked Chan to please come to LA and visit me. I told him I was feeling weak, that I had a doctor's appointment and I was scared. I hoped this would prompt him to feel obligated to come so I could make sure he was okay. He promised to come the next week.

Three days later - Los Angeles May 21, 1993

I lay in bed and something woke me up at seven a.m., then the phone rang,

"Hello?" I said.

"Hi, honey, it's Dick. Chan's dead, he died last night," Dick Crane said.

"What?" I said, in shock.

"Chan died last night honey. He killed himself. He was a very confused kid."

"What?" I found myself on my feet. "What? What? I'm in shock. I'm in shock. I don't know what I'm doing. I'm in shock," I told him. I couldn't breathe. I was hyperventilating and walking around in circles in my big white room.

"There is a plane ticket waiting for you on Delta, can you get to the airport?" he asked matter-of-factly.

"Yes, yes. I'm in shock, I'm in shock." I was pleading with him. I was in shock, that's all I could say. I was in shock. "Where's Daddy?" I cried.

"He's on his way to Kentucky, you have to call your mom." Then we hung up.

I don't remember much else except I called my friend and told her my brother died and I needed to get to the airport. I walked around my apartment in circles. I got in the shower and I was still going in circles, sobbing and gagging. Then I called my Mom. I told her Chan was with Daddy Gene.

He didn't kill himself. It was a horrible tragic accident but I was left with that image for a day before I found out what really happened. He was in Las Vegas, in my dad's condo on the golf course behind the Hilton. He was with a twenty-one year old girl he had flown in from

Kentucky. The phone bill hadn't been paid so it was turned off, so was the TV. They had resorted to watching the same DVD's over and over, *Bugsy* and *The Last Boy Scout*. He had been smoking crack and drinking bottles of Vodka. She had been rollerblading around the complex.

He was on a binge, spiraling downward, spinning out of control. He had shaved his head a few days before, and was bald for the first time in his life. The girl said he liked it and danced around in front of the mirror. He met a Kentucky friend, Joe Marcum, at the Sports Book at noon that day. Joe had been sober for five years. They talked. Joe had a Coke. Chan had a Heineken. They discussed his going back to treatment. Chan said he was ready. "I'll either sober up, get locked up, or get covered up." Then he told Joe, "Jesus Christ, I can't believe I have to go back to that fucking place." That was how the day began. This is how it ended…

"Uh, this is Detective Young, taking a voluntary statement, that number is 930520-1880. Title of this report will be dead body/self inflicted. Date, time occurred 5-20-93… 21-22 hours. Location of occurrence, 744 Tam O'Shanter, Las Vegas, Nevada. Name of person giving statement, first name Tracy, middle name Anne, last name Farr. Date of birth 8-6-of 71. Persons present, Detective Young P- number 3166 and Tracy Farr, date is 5-20-93 time is 23-22."

"Tracy, you understand this statement is being tape-recorded and is being done so with your consent?"

"Yes," Tracy said in her husky Kentucky accent.

"What I'd like you to do is tell me what has been going on between you and Joseph, both tonight and the past few days."

"Um, I came out here Sunday to visit him, and… um, we have been hanging out, he has been drinking all day today. You want me to talk about today?"

"Start with… with today," he replied.

"Um. Okay," she began gravely. *"We got up… he started drinking, we went to the casino, bet a game and he won that game and then we went back to here, laid out, he drank some more. And then we went back to the casino and met his friend."*

"Do you remember which casino that was?"

"We've been to tons of casinos."

"But do you remember which casino?"

"We met his friend at?"

"Right."

She took a deep breath, *"let's see… Hilton!"* she remembered.

"At the Hilton. Okay, now this friend, you gave me his name earlier, that's Joseph Marcum?"

"Right, right. He was havin' a horse run that was at Churchill Downs and we bet on that. And then um… Joe left, he left and we went to the Mirage and hung out at the pool there and then we were on our way home, and that's when Chan went downtown."

"Okay, you call him Chan?"

"Right, but I'm referring to Joseph," she whispered.

"Joseph Chandler," he stated.

"Right, right, Joseph Chandler," she said hesitantly. *"But I will call him Chan, 'cause that's all I know him as. And um, he bought some drugs, some crack, I guess, and brought it back here."*

"Did you see the person that he bought it from?"

"Yeah…." She said nervously.

"Was it a white person or a black person?"

"Black person."

"Would you recognize this person if you saw him again?"

"Possibly, but like… he went back down there with a gun and…" she started to get out of breath.

"Okay, do you know the area where he went to buy this at? Was it near the hotels, away from the hotels?"

"*I'm not…*" *she began. "It's Freedom or Freedmont or…*"

"*Freemont?*"

"*Freemont!*" *she confirmed. "That's what he called it.*"

"*Do you remember what it was near, what type of buildings?*"

"*Umm, he just took a right, right here,*" *she motioned to the guard gate.*

"*Okay, are you familiar with Las Vegas at all?*"

"*No, I've never been here before,*" *she said.*

"*Okay, so now you say he purchased some crack, do you know what that is?*" *he asked.*

"*Cocaine,*" *she drawled.*

"*Okay, I mean but do you know that's what he bought, I mean did he tell you that's what he bought? Did you see it?*"

"*I saw it.*"

"*And what did it look like?*"

"*Little… white… square crystals.*"

"*And do you remember how much he paid for it?*"

"*Thirty-five, forty dollars.*"

"*And you saw him give this person money?*"

"*Yes.*"

"*All right, then you guys came back here to the apartment, or rather the condo.*" "*Right. And um he did it and um…*"

"*Okay, when you say he did it, he smoked it? Or… did what with it?*"

"*Smoked it. He had some kind of a pipe deal.*" *Her voice trailed off, tired and lost.*

"*What did that pipe look like?*"

"*It's in there… It's round and it has a little…*"

"*What's it made out of?*"

"*Glass,*" *she whispered.*

"*Glass. Now that's the one that's lying in the kitchen? It's sitting on the kitchen counter?*"

"*I guess. He was in the kitchen.*"

"*Okay, he did it in there. Now did you handle this crack pipe at all?*"

"*Mmm hmm.*" *She was barely audible.*

"*You did. When did you hold that?*" *he asked.*

"*I looked at it…*"

"*Did you smoke any of this crack?*"

"*No.*"

"*All right,*" *he said, fatherly.* "*Go ahead.*"

"*And then he said he was leaving to go downtown and he asked me if I wanted to go and I said no, and… I … then I stayed here.*"

"*Did he tell you why he was going back downtown? And did you see him leave with a gun?*"

"*Mmm hmm.*"

"*Okay, so he left and he came back an hour later? And then what happened?*"

"*I guess it was an hour, I took a bath and everything and watched part of that movie so…*"

"*So he comes home…*" *he led her.*

She took another deep breath before her voice broke, "*right, and um he was just like… 'How are you doin'?' And he said, 'I went back down there and I held a gun to him.*"

She took on his frantic state, "*And he kept sayin' 'It's like in the movies!' and stuff. And he was really upset with himself because he said, 'you know this is Las Vegas, you can't do shit like that, they'll slit your throat!' and he said, 'You can die doin' stuff like that.'*"

"*So, he told you that he put the gun to this other guy's head, that he had gone downtown driving his truck, which is the one that you pointed out to me that's out front… the Toyota.*"

"*Right. He said he told the guy, 'Come here'… and the guy got in his car and I can't remember the details but he said, 'give me my money back' and Chan said the guy emptied out all his pockets and said,*"

'I'll make it up to you'… and he gave him all his crack. Did ya'll find crack?"

"Where would that be in the house?"

"I don't know, he might have thrown it away. I'm not really sure."

"Okay, what was it contained in?"

"In nothing."

"Just loose rocks?"

"Yeah." She confirmed.

"Do you know where he would normally keep that in the house?"

"I've never seen him do it before," she said softly.

"Okay, do you know where the gun was kept?" He asked.

"A couple days ago I found that crack pipe and I thought it was like a bong or something to smoke pot out of and it had all these ashes in it! I said, 'Someone put ashes in your bong,' and I dumped 'em all out and, like, tonight I found out what it was used for."

"Okay, so do you know where the gun was kept?"

"I think he keeps it in his closet, up there on the shelf."

"In the back bedroom?"

"Right."

"So he came back… and that's when he told you about all this stuff that went on downtown?" he guided her.

"Yeah, he said he had the gun and he said, 'and I put the gun up to his head like this' you know. He wasn't putting it up to my head, he was standin' up and doin' this and stuff. And he was real upset with himself and said, 'I'm gonna' put this gun up.' So he put it back in back room, I guess in the closet or wherever he puts it, and then he got the vodka out and started drinkin' that."

"That's the bottle of vodka?"

"Right."

"Okay. Did you drink any of that?" he asked her.

"Mmmm mmm."

"All right, there's an open bottle of beer in there, did you drink any of that?"

"Nope, that's his," she said.

"Okay, do you drink at all?"

"I do drink, but I..."

"Did you drink at all tonight?"

"Earlier this afternoon I had a Heineken at the casino and I had Miller Light at the pool," she told him.

"So go ahead there."

"Then he just started talkin' about things and... um... was sayin' he was upset with himself and he said, 'If I could talk to Leader,' and 'if my phone worked and I could talk to someone and they would tell me it's okay that I went down there and stood up for my rights!' He was just really upset about that. Just goin' on and on about stuff. And we were just talkin' and he was sayin' that he wanted to quit drinkin' and all this. And I said, 'Well, you know, quit. Don't drink that vodka.' And he just kept drinkin', he was doin' shots of Vodka and chasin' it with Gatorade."

"So that's what's in the plastic cup?" Detective Young asked.

"Right." Tracy said.

"Okay, so then what happened?"

"So then we were just settin' there and he said, 'I'm gonna' do the Bugsy Siegel'. He kept sayin', 'All this violence I've been watchin' Bugsy and I've been watchin' The Last Boy Scout and I just went down there and I thought it was like the movies'... and then he goes, 'I'm gonna' do the Bugsy Siegel' and um... he aaaah... went into the other room and he got his gun and I thought he took all the shells out!"

"You saw him empty the gun out on the table?"

"He opened the little silver thing, I don't know how... do they fall out? Or, I don't know, but they came out." she said.

"Did they fall out on the table?" he asked.

"No, he put them in his hand and..."

"And he set them on the table," he finished.

"And you know, at this point I thought the gun was empty!" Tracy said.

"Okay, did he close the gun back up?"

"He spun it and closed it and put it up to his head."

"Okay, and then what happened?"

"And he pulled the trigger."

"Did he say anything to you?"

"No."

"All right, now after he pulled the trigger, he fell straight to the floor?"

"Back." She said.

"Okay, now I asked you earlier and we then looked at you, and you uh, don't have any injuries other than the ones you showed us which are old. And you only have two spots of blood, it looks like on your shirt, is that correct?

"Yes," she said softly, back in her shell.

"Okay, did you wash your hands at all before the officers got here?"

"No."

"Okay, have you changed your clothes?" he asked.

"No."

"All right, now is there anything else? I'm gonna ask you this part straight up. Did you shoot the gun that killed Joseph?"

"No," she said.

"Okay, was there anyone else present other than you two?" he asked.

"No."

"And you're sure of that?"

"Yes."

"Okay, now is there anything else that we haven't talked about that you think is important?" he said gently, wrapping it up.

"No."

"Okay, is there anything else that you want to add?"
"No."
"Okay, we'll end the statement, same persons present, time is 23-24."

Joseph Daniel "Chan" Chandler Jr., Maine

Thirty-One

Los Angeles/Kentucky May 1993

I remember driving to the airport, looking out the window, dead inside. I remember throwing up in First Class on the plane flying back to Kentucky. I remember being upstairs in the Cabin with my mom and dad and Uncle Brad looking through Chan's room. My mom screamed and sobbed, grasping a bag of pictures and letters of his that she held onto like a crazy person for five days. She wouldn't stop screaming and I grabbed the huge antique mirror off the wall and threw it to the ground and it burst into a thousand pieces before I ran downstairs.

It was an open casket at St. John's church in Versailles. Chan looked really good. He looked like himself, with a smile on his face and a baseball cap on his head to cover the injury in the back. Daddy cried as he stood in the chapel and for some reason snapped pictures of him lying there. The family that worked and lived with my grandmother, Berthina, Ramon and their little girl Betsy wept and held onto the casket. Lissa, Chan's old girlfriend, ran out of the church and right into the street, oblivious to traffic, screaming and sobbing with her hands in the air. Several cars almost hit her as she ran across the street like a madwoman.

I sat silent, broken and stunned as we listened to the church service in the beautiful Episcopal Church we had gone to since we were little, the same ornate building where Chan had been an altar boy, and Mammy and Aunt Mimi sang in the choir. Chan and I spent our first years on earth going to Sunday school here, sitting in these wooden pews below the stained-glass portraits of Jesus and Mary and the Apostles.

The church was overcrowded with people. Our cousin Ben gave a eulogy. So did the preacher. Then Kentucky Basketball coach Rick Pitino got up and spoke. This seemed out of the blue to me. He knew Chan and loved my dad so he gave a touching tribute. Daddy wouldn't let Chan's best friend Leader speak because he thought he had been a bad influence. This was terribly wrong. Leader spent more time with Chan than anyone and loved him like a brother. His heart had been shattered and he should have been able to say what he wanted to say. But what holds weight with Daddy is what holds weight with Daddy, and famous sports figures always have, no matter what the occasion.

I remember the long line of cars all the way down Versailles road for ten miles from the church to the Pisgah cemetery. Hundreds of faces we hadn't seen in years and some we had never seen before. Girls sobbing, we didn't know who they were. Mamma was pleased to see the Versailles cops stand in the middle of the street for Chan, directing traffic. She hated them. She blamed them. She wanted them to see who he really was. She wanted them put out by this amazing display of love.

Thirty-Two

*"When you're by yourself and there's no
one else, you just have yourself and you
tell yourself just to hold on..."*

J OHN L ENNON

Los Angeles June 1993

I wandered around in Chan's Toyota 4-Runner from bar to A.A. meeting to rooftop listening to what was in his CD player. Mick Jagger sang, *"Oh, am I running in a race? Oh, I'm not getting any place. Oh, can I make it? I'm a wandering spirit. Yes I am a restless soul. Wandering spirit. There's no place that I can call my home."*

The song played like a soundtrack. I saw Chan driving through the desert, the lone opening guitar groovily edging forward, a perfect backdrop for the ever-changing environment of a trip across the country. Half of me was up in the sky. The other half was driving down La Brea Blvd in Hollywood. The air was pasty yellow from the gutters to the heavens.

I was detached from my surroundings but an integral part of everything. Every silly form of humanity and invasive mismatched building was on my side, the side of the living. I spotted two young guys heading wherever the day took them and asked if they knew where I could get pot. They hopped in the car and directed me to a building on the sketchy, gang infested side of Hollywood Blvd., to the neighborhood hipsters only frequent if they want to get really good Thai food.

I followed them into a building, up three flights of stairs and down a long, narrow, pee stained hallway. Passing matchbox rooms with bunk beds, people poked their heads out and kids crossed in front of us in diapers. We ducked into one of the closet sized apartments and walked the three steps to the other end of it. We climbed out the window and onto the roof. As I stepped out onto the asphalt, with the dirty skyline as a backdrop, I spotted what must be our destination. A heavyset Hispanic man sat in a folding chair with a duffle bag and baseball bat at his feet and an old school ghetto blaster in reaching distance. He was humorless and silent. He rolled a joint and passed it to the spectacle that I was. He followed that up with a beer from his duffle bag, which I accepted.

I told him about Chan. He responded in kind with a sympathetic nod and turned up the music. The three of us started to dance, the head honcho stayed in his folding chair bobbing his head. It was the first time I had smiled since Chan left.

I made my way down, back to Chan's/my car and drove back to my apartment on Sycamore. I went to my therapist, Phoebe's office the next day. I told her what I had been doing. She said I was trying to kill myself like my brother. I told her I wasn't. I was just trying to survive the day. I thought that was what therapy was for, to tell them what you had been doing and talk about it.

Phoebe had been telling me to go to meetings, but I cursed A.A. people for not understanding. I thought they would never be able to grasp what kind of loss had taken place. What a brilliant, soulful, intelligent human being had been lost.

"We'll never know because Chan pulled the trigger and killed himself. We'll never see his potential because he killed himself." Through the fog, I heard.

I was mad. I didn't care how screwed up on drugs and alcohol he was, Russian roulette or whatever. It may have been an accident but he knew there was one bullet in that gun. One chance it would blow his brains out and he took that chance. He put the hideous killing machine to his head and pulled the trigger. Now that is a fuck you to God and everyone. I was furious at him for leaving me here alone. It was mean to pull the trigger. I had been thinking spiritually, albeit miserably and vomiting, but spiritually. I had been thinking, maybe it was supposed to happen. Now he gets to be an angel, a wonderful guardian angel. But he took away my guardian angel on earth. He took my angel away from me and left me to do this alone. I was lonely, still in shock and so angry that Chan would selfishly destroy his beautiful, shining light, taking it away from me forever.

Phoebe said that my recent behavior was my own big fuck you to the universe. She said dancing on rooftops with gang members in the middle of the day, drinking and smoking pot was one of the biggest insults to life there was. She didn't understand that I was trying to have a life, I really was. I was just really confused about how to get one, now more than ever. I knew I had to be sober to be happy, or at least clear and coherent. I just preferred not to be. *Only a phase, these dark café days...* I'll be dammed if I wasn't getting more than my fair share of these phases, but I was trying to not compare lives and paths and get on with my own path to some sort of something.

Phoebe went for the tough love approach. She said I couldn't come back until I had 30 days of sobriety. At this point, I think my brother had been gone for about three weeks and it was pretty much the only thing I had talked about in therapy the previous year. I worried about him constantly and agonized over the thought he might not be around. She knew I had tried indefatigably to save his life. Now my worst fear was realized and her only parting words were, "get 30 days."

"So, you don't want me to come back next Thursday?" I asked her.

"No," she said. "Come back when you have 30 days. Your brother dying really knocked the breath out of you, and you didn't have much breath to begin with."

I gave her a hug and wandered out of her house. I stumbled onto the street and into the smoggy LA late afternoon sun with one less string attaching me to the earth. I got back into Chan's/my car and pulled onto La Brea and drove back to my apartment.

I don't know how I got through those first few months. I sat in my dark apartment like an old hermit, crying. When the occasional guest entered my dwelling, I mumbled thanks for the flowers or plant and said good-bye. All I could do was crawl back into my hole.

I had a dream one night and I know it was a visitation. I was driving around in his truck and the car phone rang. I picked up and it was Chan. He sounded so vibrant and happy, "Hey! It's me! This is how it works!" I don't remember exactly all he said but he sounded great. I was frozen. My body was frozen, like I was scared to death. I can't explain it. I have never felt anything like it before or since but I was awake. "All you have to do is love," he told me. "That's all there is. All you have to do is love everyone. Let me be with you," he said. "Please, let me be with you."

I woke up like I had seen a ghost. My body hurt from, not fear, but something like it. Happy tears were streaming down my face. It was Chan. He made contact.

Chan and Erin, at the Cabin, Versailles, Kentucky

His car was stolen from my street a few months later. Somehow, I began to come alive again and I came at life with a vengeance. I started to get little TV and film parts, which made me an actual working actress. With Chan gone, most of my insecurity or self-involvement seemed pointless. My heart had been broken so deeply that everything else was frankly easy to get through. Like that movie said, *"Be careful of damaged people... they know they can survive."*

Thirty-Three

"It's a mean old world, heavy in need. That
big machine is just a-picking up speed..."

GILLIAN WELCH

Kentucky June 2003

It officially sank in that we were not going to come up with
the money to move to New York. My dreams of cobblestone
streets and romantic walks to tiny cafés had fallen by the wayside.
Nothing magical was going to happen this time to make thousands
of dollars appear in my pocket. We were at a standstill. I suppose
we should have been content, for all intents and purposes we were
very comfortable. Daddy was certainly happy, with two live-in
maids at his beck and call to cook, clean, find the remote and fix
the ever-cryptic digital cable. He needed lots of attention and we
were a captive audience.

"PEST CONTROL MAN!" He screamed bloody murder
one morning from the bottom of the stairs, "PEST CONTROL
MAN!!!! PEEEEEEST CONTROOOOOL MAAAAAN!!!" I ran
out of my room in my pajamas and stood at the top of the stairs.

"Daddy, what?" I asked, startled and confused.

"The pest control man is here." He looked calmly up at me.

"Well? He knows what he's doing, doesn't he?" I asked.

"Yeah, I guess." He shrugged and turned around. "I just thought you would want to know."

I had to get out of there. My father had spent his whole life having other people do everything for him. Now without his 'lackeys' it was my job to pick up the slack. Even making a Slim Fast shake was too complex. When I patiently showed him the three simple steps of putting milk, powder and ice into the blender, he shook his head and turned away, "I... I don't know about this," he mumbled. "I'm goin' back in my room."

When boredom set in, and with my father it always did, he made a sport of baiting and teasing me. I cooked and cleaned until it was time to cook and clean again. Daddy picked and picked until it was time for him to pick and pick again. I walked on eggshells, constantly trying to please and continuously disappointing.

When I played Chrissy in David Rabe's, *In the Boom Boom Room*, Ken Kercheval played my father. There was a haunting scene where he sat with me in the garden.

"See, I'm gonna feed this plant," he delicately held out a plant and studied it. *"I'm gonna give it lots of water and plenty of sunshine and I'm gonna watch it grow. Then I'm gonna eat it. Givin' somethin' life gives you that right, don't you think? It'll be interesting."*

This landed like a punch in the gut. That was my dad and people pleasing, dreaming, desperate, and damaged Chrissy was me. I could not live with my father much longer or he would consume my whole life. He would eat up my head, my heart and my soul and there would be nothing left, and he thought this was his right.

Sam and I used to be happy, motivated, passionate people, excited about our work and romantic with each other. What happened? When did we take this incredibly wrong turn? Were our creative lives finished? Had we experienced our fun and now it was time to get back on the farm?

When I started going into these depressive, what-happened-to-my-life crying jags, Daddy kept his distance. He hadn't seen this side of me, at least to this extent and it freaked him out. He started to lean heavier on Sam. He attributed my mental collapse to being spoiled. He couldn't believe I wasn't happy in the Cabin. He couldn't understand how we could possibly want to go to New York or even back to LA with no money. I suppose the plan was to sit tight and wait but I was underground, spitting up dirt and trying to climb out.

It was painfully obvious we had to leave if I planned on having one nerve ending left. We couldn't afford New York and we were both too frazzled for that endeavor anyway. We knew how to be broke in LA, or at least we were going to find out. We decided to make a U-turn.

The minute this decision was made, I got my spirit back. I started dancing around the Cabin and rapping, *"We're goin' back to Cali, to Cali, to Cali. We're goin' back to Cali..."*

Daddy slouched over and whimpered, "My baby's leaving me."

I spent the next two weeks trying to come up with money to get us out of there. I figured we could hit the road with about $1500 dollars. I had already saved up a thousand and hidden it in my underwear drawer anticipating a getaway. I had a garage sale to try to get the rest. I drug most of my belongings out to the front yard: Betsy Johnson dresses, leopard coats, and a bunch of other stuff that no one in Versailles had any use for. I placed a stereo, several purses and some feather boas on a long table. A CD rack and a pair of silver candelabras stood on the grass. I made one hundred and fifty bucks that day.

"Hey honey! How's it goin'?" Daddy screamed perched on a high stool on the front porch of the Cabin. He was drinking Scotch and smoking cigars with a few buddies and wobbled up to the curb handing me a beer, "I'm gonna' put up a lemonade stand and join you in a few minutes." Then he forced his friends to buy something.

It was only a matter of getting the cash to drive across the country, and a tiny bit for our first weeks in LA. We needed just enough to get us to familiar territory and we could take it from there. Our friends, Gina and Mark promised a room in their house in West Hollywood and had arranged jobs for us at the Ahmanson Theatre. Connie offered up the couch of her apartment in Los Feliz and said we could stay as long as we needed. There was a light at the end of the tunnel.

First I had to raise more cash. It was clearly up to me because Sam was paralyzed by the drama and glued to the TV set. I frantically went around the Cabin videotaping antique mirrors, dressers, and an old jukebox, basically anything I thought I could get in the car and sell. This was all way sketchy, since my dad was keeping close tabs on every little thing after my big redecorating experiment. He might have missed a gigantic mirror from the wall. I ditched that idea pretty quickly and started hunting for smaller things to sell. I remembered some jewelry my grandmother had given me and I rushed to the pawnshop making another four hundred dollars.

The next day we began to stuff everything we could fit into the car and the small U-Haul attached to the back. I thought I was being conservative, only taking one tub of personal things, journals, pictures, tapes and a sushi set we got for our wedding. I thought I was being so good that it would be okay to bring six tubs of books. This infuriated Sam but my books were simply too comforting for me to leave behind. I could replace furniture but it would be forever to replace all my books. Anyway, he got to take his speakers, and wires, and guitars, and keyboards so I figured I could have my books.

When I asked him to stuff our gigantic sleigh bed in the tiny U-Haul he wanted to commit Hari Kari. I wanted to at least have a bed when we pulled back into town. I heard him mention something about a blow-up bed and I panicked. Sam transformed into a madman, screaming and cursing as he stuffed the huge headboard into the truck, breaking off irreplaceable parts with every violent shove.

My father stumbled into the kitchen looking for his car keys. He had taken some pill and was not making sense. I noticed he was slurring on the phone, attempting to transfer money into my account. Practically falling asleep standing up, he mentioned some meeting and headed for the car. I reached for his arm in horror and told him he could not drive. "I'll be fine. I'll just keep the windows rolled down and the music up."

I needed to help Sam load the truck but now I obviously had to drive my dad to this campaign meeting he was determined to make. I was completely anxiety-ridden and petrified, nervous and scared to be forced out in the elements. I had no idea where we were going and wasn't used to the country roads. I was sure I would get lost coming home. Daddy fell asleep in the car with a cigar hanging out of his mouth. It slowly tipped all the way over and started to burn his shirt. When we got to the campaign office in Frankfort, we found out he was two hours early. He insisted on staying anyway and wobbled into the office. As I watched him stagger in, I put my head down on the wheel and wept.

I was abandoning my fragile father. It was traumatizing to witness Daddy drive himself into the ground. Still I had to keep moving. I drove back to Versailles sobbing and chanting for God to help me. Arriving back at the Cabin, I was met by my hostile, cursing husband still stuffing the U-Haul.

Daddy got home around five. Whatever he had taken had thankfully worn off. We could have all used a good nights sleep but it was time to set up for the barbeque I planned for Aunt Toss, Uncle Ben, Whit and Mathew. Trying one last time in Kentucky to be a good hostess, I put out chips and salsa, potato salad, sliced tomatoes and onions for the hamburgers.

Daddy sat on the rocking chair with big tears in his blue eyes, whimpering, "Remember when we would go see Wayne Newton and you would sing to me, *Daddy don't you walk so fast?* I don't want my Erin to go… I don't want my baby to go."

"I can't live with my parents." I told him. "You or Mamma! It's not personal!"

"Why not?" he said, "I did."

Thirty-Four

"River stay away from my door..."

MORT DIXON

Kentucky June 2003

The car was packed up and we were ready to go. I felt strangely calm the night before Sam and I left the cabin, not frantic to get away, not nervous or sick. I was sore and tired from the emotional last days but mainly I felt content and like I needed to rest. I felt hopeful for the future and sure a lot of it would be good. The whole experience was crazier than I could have imagined. Now it was over. Time to move on.

I went upstairs early, took a shower and got into bed. Sam brought up popcorn and Cokes. The atmosphere was calm. Whit and Mathew came over and climbed into bed with us. Whit did our astrological charts and informed me that all of the insanity was soon to be over. He said if we could just hold on until Christmas, it looked like things were going to turn around. It was only June and that sounded far off but I was taking what I could get. He told me that this 'journey home' had been an important life lesson and something I had to do. Mathew promised to come visit us in Los Angeles if he could meet David Carradine.

It was the most relaxed visit I had with my cousins in the whole six months we had been in Kentucky. It was pouring rain outside and we were all in bed, my family and me. It certainly felt like the tough part was over.

"You are a travelin' show." Daddy said as we walked to the car the next morning, "I feel sorry for Sam."

He hugged and kissed me and slipped some money into my hand. As we drove down the long driveway in our black Dodge Durango, Daddy yelled one last piece of advice. "Have fun, okay? Enjoy life!"

"What?" I yelled out the window.

"I SAID, ENJOY YOURSELF!!!!!" he screamed at the top of his lungs. "DO YOU KNOW WHAT THAT MEANS?!" he snapped accusingly. "HAVE A GOOD TIME!!!" Then he disappeared out of frame.

I felt a mixture of guilt, exhaustion and relief. Sam and I hardly spoke a word that first day of traveling, we were both shell-shocked and beat. I decided I knew what the Beat Poets were talking about. I knew what they meant by beat. Not conquered, but beat. I didn't care, truly living day to day with only a few belongings. I had no idea or concern for what the future held.

I stared out the window. It was so refreshing to see something other than that one block of Elm Street, to have a choice of places to eat besides the Sweet Potato. So happy to not have a gaggle of people in my face telling me how to live my life or how I had screwed up in the past. What a tremendous relief it was not to hear about how scary the world is and to stay 'where I belong.'

Versailles had begun to feel like the Bermuda Triangle and I thought we would never make it out alive. Now, to be living from one gas station to the next, one McDonald's to the next, one Best Western to the next, was heavenly. We were free and it was beautiful. I started to laugh again and with every mile of road, my old self crept back into my bones.

I was happy.

Thirty-Five

"Singin' hard times ain't gonna rule my mind.
Hard times ain't gonna rule my mind, Bessie. Hard
times ain't gonna rule my mind no more..."

GILLIAN WELCH

Los Angeles June 2003

We drove into Los Angeles about three in the afternoon. With the murky skyline finally in sight, we squealed with joy. We were home and it was a wonderful life.

"Merry Christmas movie house!" Sam screamed.

"Merry Christmas, you old Savings and Loan!" I laughed.

We powered up the 101 freeway, past downtown toward the Hollywood Hills and with colorful stucco houses covered with bougainvillea on our left and palm trees and the Hollywood sign on our right, we exited the freeway. We drove down Franklin Avenue wide-eyed and innocent and took it all in. I embraced with love every jet black haired, body pierced lesbian, every soul-patched, 70s clothes-wearing hipster and every blonde-haired, big boobed, big-lipped stripper on Sunset Blvd. Viva la difference! Thank God for self-expression. Thank God for nonjudgement. Thank God for this city.

We landed in a tiny apartment in Hollywood, the only place that would take us with very little money and horrible credit. We were also traveling a bit lighter having been robbed on the way. Staying at my cousin Katie's in Scottsdale, Arizona on the way, our U-Haul was broken into and the bandits made off with two of Sam's guitars, his speakers, keyboard and my one tub of personal belongings. It was the only one that was really important to me, with old journals and irreplaceable videotapes of plays I had done. Upon discovering this Sam kicked the U-Haul then we got back in the car and hardly mentioned it again… we were already spent. Sam joked with our friends later, "I lost all my music equipment but we still have every book Erin has ever read."

We moved into a converted monastery run by an Israeli gypsy named Daniel. I was at home on this hillside in Beachwood Canyon. This is exactly where I wanted to be. It was a tiny studio apartment but I felt safe. I used to live in a great old 1920s house across the way and my window looked out over this place encrusted in the mountain. More than once, after a night of debauchery, I prayed for forgiveness and pictured my whole body curled up in this mountain, sleeping soundly, a part of the land. Now I truly was one of the *Ladies of the Canyon*.

Our small bathroom was suspended over the Monastery of the Angels and I could see the cloistered nuns walking in prayer and contemplation. I lay in the tiny bathtub with pink candles and lavender bubbles and prayed to St. Germaine, the patron saint of the unwanted. My legs hung over the edge of our small white loveseat and I listened on the phone to Penny Calcina, a healer in South Carolina. Tears of joy streamed down my face as she chanted and sang, channeling old Indian Shamans on the other end of the line. I scrubbed every inch of the tile floor and dusted every surface with Pledge as I listened to Jimmy Scott sing *When You Wish Upon a Star*. I opened the windows and let the breeze flow in while I perfected our sweet little hillside home.

I was at once totally floored as to what had happened and completely at home and comfortable. Gone were the anxieties and desperation about my career, replaced with a thankfulness to be alive with my sanity intact. They say the universe will knock you to your knees if you are on the wrong track. The universe and I are on strong speaking terms. It has knocked me down more than a few times to show me in no uncertain terms that I was heading in the wrong direction.

Thirty-Six

"But tomorrow may rain so I'll follow the sun..."

THE BEATLES

Los Angeles April 2004

My dad died on my birthday, April 27th, one year after we left Kentucky. He called the night before and sang Happy Birthday and asked me what I wanted, "how about a new car?"

"I think that's a little extravagant, Daddy," I smiled, bundled up on the couch. "I want you and me and Mamma and Sam to go on a trip! We'll go to Paris or something, wouldn't that be amazing? Or maybe we'll go to some beachy place, the Bahamas or something just to hang out."

"We'll do it. That's done," he said. "We'll go on Tony Novelli's boat later this summer. But give me a week and I'm going to figure out what I'm going to get you for your birthday."

He sounded a little tired and more subdued. He died that night in his sleep. He had a heart attack, or his heart just stopped. He just went to sleep and didn't wake up. He went on to the other side. "He left," as Mamma puts it.

It was Father's Day, June 20th when I left Las Vegas for the last time. The first day of summer in the 108-degree heat, Sam and I drove across the desert in my dad's gold Nissan Pathfinder, packed with boxes of papers and framed pictures from his house. For the last time we drove away from the condo where Daddy lived for 20 years. The house that still looked like he had moved in a month ago. The house where I had lived off and on since I was ten. The house my brother died in, the house where I was never fully comfortable, the house that personified transience. The house I will never miss at all.

I miss my dad. I miss driving out to the desert with him blaring the music and singing the words with tears in his eyes. I miss us— Chan, Daddy and me—us. I am the last one standing from that crazy desert life, the long Las Vegas detour that changed us forever.

There is something so familiar and soothing about driving in the middle of the desert looking out over the Sierra Nevada Mountains. Listening to the Eagles, staring at the sage and cactus below bronze colored mountains that touched the wide blue sky, I am aware of my priceless education of life on the road. Proud of this firmly secured love for good, loud music, beautiful scenery and the feeling of 'gettin' some road under us' as Daddy would say. The feeling of moving forward and moving on is burned into my soul and will never go away.

I sold the Cabin to Uncle Ben. The Cabin Daddy called our place, the Cabin that never felt like our place. The Cabin that still pulses with Chan's intense energy, from jubilation to gut-wrenching despair, the Cabin I used to go through in the dark, searching desperately in the throes of my own alcohol imbued decadence.

I let go of the pool that we swam in when we were children and all was well. I let go of the yard that I ran around in and got a bee sting when I was five, the scar still on the bottom of my foot. I let go of the devil room, and the vast dark living room. I let go of the porch, and the new wing of the Cabin with the bright bedroom, bay windows and white carpets Daddy added to make it more our own. It wasn't enough. The Cabin was much too heavy to lighten up. It still stands, unflinching, strong, dark and haunted.

I don't know exactly when Sam started hating me but I suspect it was during one of the several breakdowns I had in Kentucky. It took me so long to notice because he had been so in love with me and I never dreamed that could just vanish.

It was New Year's Day, 2004 when he walked out in the pouring rain with his bags, pretending he was going away for a trial run. He never came back and denied the affair he was having with the woman who owned the film company throughout the therapy sessions we went to after he moved out. It wasn't until later I discovered she was already pregnant.

He talked a lot about his childhood in those sessions. He told me I had abandonment issues. "And this is going to make them better?" I asked.

"You're going to keep buying furniture we can't afford and houses we can't afford," Sam repeated with his head down in those sessions. "The minute we get comfortable in one place you move us somewhere else."

I have moved every three years since I was born. He lived in one house his whole life. Maybe that had something to do with it. I exhaust myself now that I think of me, but there was somewhere I wanted to be and it wasn't where we were. "*You are a travelin' show,*" Daddy said as I packed us up to leave Kentucky. "*I feel sorry for Sam.*"

So my marriage didn't survive the storm, but all is as it should be. I guess I am a traveling show, but I love my life. I am getting stronger from the inside out and coming into my own. I talk to my mom every day now. After Paul died, she married her college sweetheart, Locky Brown. We are both shell shocked from the experience of enduring and surviving life with my father and brother, the extraordinary men in our family. Although neither of us would have it any other way.

I grew up knowing that I was the most important thing in the world to Chan and Daddy. It's a wonderful feeling to know without a doubt that you are important to another human being. With all their insanity, my brother and father loved me fully and unconditionally. The love we had for each other is rare and ingrained in my bones. I know I am blessed to have been loved like that.

Herman Melville said, "Life's a voyage that is homeward bound." I've landed, truly landed in the sweet soft spot that was inside me all along, a little shaken but I made it home.

I am reminded of what Mammy said, passing through the kitchen in her flowered house dress: *"This world, one more… then come the fireworks."* It is now many years since my brother's death in May of 1993, but I swear to you it feels like yesterday. He is still my big brother and he is still two years older than me. I can sense his eyes on me when I'm up to no good and I feel his warm embrace when I'm scared. No matter how many successes I have or how many mistakes I make, he will not be far away. I am still his baby sister and he will watch over me forever.

This is for you, Chan and Daddy. I love you both more than I can say.

THE END

A Note From the Author

I would like to offer my gratitude for all of those early readers, editors and supporters of this book who gave their time, insight and encouragement, Dr. Jane Gentry Vance, Leslie Jordan, Brandon Lo Casto, Gina East, Jim Victor, Erin Cox, Anna Mastro, Nick Cassavetes, Shawn Hatosy, Muffy Bolding, Warren Seabury, Claudia Love Mair, Martha Jane Agan, Silas House, Robin Lippincott, Nancy McCabe, Dianne Aprile, Sena Jeter Naslund, Kathleen Driscoll and the Spalding University community of writers with whom I have had the pleasure to work with. My heartfelt appreciation to the Weymouth Center for Arts and Humanities in North Carolina for several stints as writer in residence, which gave me the time and silence I needed to move the book along. I also thank Juni Mashayekhi, Connie Blankenship, Jenny Marshall and Matt Flanders for their undying friendship, I love you deeply.

Finally, I thank my brother and father, to whom this book is dedicated and offer my deepest gratitude to my extraordinary mother for her beauty inside and out, showing me a softer, more stable way of being.

A Note About the Author

Erin Chandler holds an MFA in Creative Writing from Spalding University and a Masters in Theatre from the University of Kentucky. Her play *June Bug Versus Hurricane* was produced at the Lost Studio in Los Angeles. Her poetry and short stories have been published in *Public Republic Magazine* and *Lexington Poetry Anthology*. Erin's work as a stage actress garnered honors such as *Best Actress Dramalogue Award* for David Rabe's *In the Boom Boom Room*. Accolades for film include *Best Ensemble* and *Best Script – Los Angeles Independent Film Fest* for *Lost in the Pershing Point Hotel*. Other film and TV credits include *Fear and Loathing in Las Vegas*, *The Net, Dead Husbands* and *Chicago Hope*. Erin continues to write, teach and occasionally act. She lives in Versailles, Kentucky with two dogs, a cat, and a fellow who wishes to forever be exempt from the written word.